LUNCH!

LUNCH!

Flavorful, Colorful, Powerful Lunch Bowls to Reclaim Your Midday Meal

Olivia Mack McCool

DOVETAIL

D

DOVETAIL

Published by Dovetail in New York, NY.
Dovetail is the publishing imprint of W&P, a division of Very Great Inc.

For details or ordering information, contact the publisher at the address below or email
info@dovetail.press.

Dovetail
52 Mercer Street, 3rd Floor
New York, NY 10013

www.dovetail.press

Library of Congress Cataloging-in-Publication data is on file with the publisher.
ISBN: 978-0-9996612-5-3
First printing, September 2018
Printed in China
10 9 8 7 6 5 4

Contents

Introduction

It's been said many a time that breakfast is the most important meal of the day. But is it? Does it give you the energy you need to get through the dreaded 4 p.m. staff meeting? Or something to look forward to while running yet another morning errand? No, that's lunch.

Lunch has the power to be either our midday savior or make us want to crawl under the desk for a nap. We've all made the wrong, only-satisfying-in-the-moment choice for lunch and regretted it about 30 minutes later when we couldn't keep our eyes open and had to guzzle a caffeinated drink just to make it through the rest of the day. As a food stylist, I spend lots of long days on my feet on photo sets. When lunchtime rolls around, I need food that will fuel and energize me as opposed to slow me down. To combat the temptations from the catering table, which is usually filled with sandwiches and cheesecake, I often bring my own lunch to work. I know that whatever I bring is going to be more nutritious and most likely tastier. And, the fact that I'm not making food choices when I'm already starving sets me up for better eating.

Most of us aren't likely to have a personal chef pack our lunch every day, so wouldn't it be ideal if someone just provided you with weekly menus for wholesome, light lunches that will make you feel great? Lunches you can pack up in a bowl or other portable containers and eat anywhere, indoors or outdoors, at home or at the office? Lunches that look and taste impressive, but that you made in a snap without having to suddenly become a savvy home cook or a kitchen goddess? Lunches that not only teach you how to eat better, but

also show you how easy it is to plan your meals ahead of time and waste less food?

That's exactly what I give you with this book: an easy-to-follow guide to 10 weeks of homemade, healthy, and delicious lunch recipes, which can be used consecutively (to build a habit of planning ahead) or sporadically (when you need them most). I've come up with a unique menu for each week that highlights three main ingredients, which are spun and combined into balanced lunch bowls. At the beginning of each chapter, there's a grocery list that you can use when you're shopping for perishables and stocking your pantry with basics. Then on Sundays, you'll spend about two hours in the kitchen preparing for the week ahead. During the week, you'll only have to do simple prep and assembly (and maybe roast a veggie here or there on Wednesday night). All the recipes make lunches for one person. Cooking for more than one? Recipes can easily be doubled to accommodate your lucky mate.

If food waste is something weighing heavily on your mind (and wallet), this book can help you cook more efficiently to reduce the amount of food you end up throwing out. There's nothing worse than having a whole bunch of mint rotting in your refrigerator because a recipe called for a handful of leaves, and then you couldn't find a way to use the rest. In an effort to curtail the habit of discarding all those unused bags of brown, mushy, and sometimes unrecognizable fruits, vegetables, and herbs, this model provides a sustainable way to shop and cook. It also offers ideas about new ways to use your favorite ingredients.

I developed these recipes with the intention of packing your diet with a rich array of colorful ingredients to create filling and nutrient-dense meals. You'll find the bowls are heavy on the vegetables and supplemented with healthy grains, whole-milk dairy, and some meat and seafood—whole foods and everything else in moderation. If you're trying to improve your health by eating a cleaner diet, bringing these vibrant lunches to work is going to keep that momentum going.

In addition to being more satisfying than takeout, the lunches you make at home will cost less than anything similar at a trendy fast casual joint. So throw away your punch card from the pricey salad place down the street—you've got something awesome waiting for you.

How to Use This Book

The layout of this cookbook may seem a bit foreign at first. This is no ordinary cookbook, and that's a good thing! Everything is laid out step by step to help you feel organized and ready for your weeks of amazing lunch bowls. In preparation for the week ahead, skim over the recipes and grocery lists to familiarize yourself with the ingredients you'll be using.

Shopping

Each chapter starts with a grocery list that spells out exactly what you'll need for a week's worth of lunch bowls. The lists don't include kosher salt, black pepper, or white sugar; those should always be in your pantry. It's wise to take a glance at the list a few days before you head out to the store, because on occasion, there might be an ingredient that you'll need to buy online or in a specialty store. Of course, not every grocery store is created equal, and sometimes you might not be able to find something that's called for. Substitutions are welcome!

Prepping

The chapters are designed so that you do most of your cooking for the week on Sunday, and those recipes come first in the chapter. Start your Sunday prep with a clean kitchen and empty sink or dishwasher (if you have one) to streamline the process. Give yourself two hours to make the recipes and prep the week's ingredients. If you spend time making some of the key elements before the week starts, it's much easier to pull off five lunch bowls. A few chapters have recipes that are meant to be prepped on Wednesday night so they'll be fresh for Thursday's and Friday's bowls. Glass jars and containers are great for storing all your grains, veggies, and dressings.

Assembling

If you're not a morning person, like 99% of people, spend a few minutes the evening before assembling your lunch bowl so there's nothing left to chance. There are a few tricks to keeping everything fresh, crisp, and tasty (you'll find them in the form of tips throughout). If you're using avocado, consider waiting until the morning to place it on your salad and squeezing a little lemon or lime juice over it to keep it from turning brown. To separate a salad in the bottom of a bowl from something like a flatbread on top, cut a round piece of parchment paper to use as a divider. All the lunches in this book are perfect for transporting in ceramic or glass containers. Try to avoid plastic containers; not only are glass and ceramic a better option for your health, but those materials also elevate the ritual of lunch to an event that's worth pausing for. I recommend investing in a high-quality sealable and portable bowl because you can layer your ingredients in an efficient way (for instance, the dressing for a salad stays in the bottom of the bowl until you're ready to toss it) and the bowl shape works beautifully for the recipes you'll find in this book.

In the Pantry

Having a well-stocked pantry makes cooking a breeze. But what's even more important is knowing what to do with all those ingredients on the shelves, learning what they can do for you, and giving them a role in your cooking repertoire. Throughout the book, you might come across foods and spices that are new to you, or perhaps learn how to use ingredients you're not used to cooking with. My hope is that you discover great ways to use your pantry items and put a dent in your spice reserves.

✴ Grains ✴

The building blocks of a great lunch, grains add heft, and some of the time they can be super nutrient dense. If you buy them in bulk, transfer them to an airtight container and store in a cool, dark place like a pantry. They'll last for several months, if not a year.

Couscous and Pasta

Both are made from either durum or semolina wheat and have relatively short cooking times (at least compared to other grains). Look for pasta that's made from durum wheat and is a product of Italy. It may be slightly more expensive, but its texture is superior by far.

Farro, Freekeh, and Wheat Berries

All three grains are the whole kernels of different types of wheat. They're high in fiber and good sources of nutrients such as vitamin B, magnesium, and zinc. All three have similar textures and tastes but vary in cooking times.

Quinoa

Whatever color (white, red, mixed) you choose, the varieties all taste pretty much the same and are an excellent source of fiber and vitamin B (energy boost!). Quinoa also contains all nine essential amino acids (protein), which aid in building muscle, fat loss, and brain function, among other important benefits.

Rice

White rice is rice that has been milled and has had its bran layer and germ removed. Brown rice is the whole grain, so it's slightly more nutritious; it's also chewier and takes longer to cook than its white counterpart. Black rice, which has been increasing in popularity, has the most fiber and antioxidants of any rice variety, plus a really nice texture. If you've never tried it, go for it!

Rice Noodles

These come in all shapes and sizes. Made from rice and water, they are cooked by being soaked in hot water. Rice noodles are a great canvas for vegetables and strongly flavored dressings and broths.

✸ Oils, Sauces, and Vinegars ✸

These will make your dishes come to life. The rich fat plus the zing of acid or strong flavor can make a salad or grain bowl greater than the sum of its parts.

Avocado Oil and Grapeseed Oil

Both of these oils are great for high-heat cooking and in dishes where you don't want a strongly flavored oil. They are the more nutritious of the neutral tasting oils. Avocado oil can be a little pricey, but contains a lot of healthy fats. I call for both in the book, and you can even use them interchangeably.

Extra Virgin Olive Oil

Save this oil for making dressings or drizzling on things. When cooking with it, use low to medium heat to get the most of its flavor and health benefits—high heat kills both.

Fish Sauce

Like some cheeses, fish sauce smells terrible but tastes amazing. Used in many Asian cultures, it adds an otherworldly deliciousness to dressings, soups, and vegetables.

Soy Sauce

Oh, how I love soy sauce. It adds both saltiness and umami to anything it touches. Tamari, aka gluten-free soy sauce, is a great option if you're concerned about your gluten intake.

Tahini

This paste made from sesame seeds is widely used in Middle Eastern and Mediterranean cooking. But lucky for us, it's gaining shelf space in American supermarkets too. Mixed with yogurt, lemon, and garlic, it makes a delicious, luxurious sauce.

Toasted Sesame Oil

Used in small amounts, this oil imparts that "Why does this taste so good?" flavor. It's very strong, so be sparing when pouring it out.

Vinegars

White wine, red wine, rice wine, balsamic, and apple cider vinegar are the ones you'll find in this book. But the options are endless. A drizzle of vinegar can take a dish from just okay to OMG yum.

✳ Spices and Seasoning ✳

When I was growing up, the only spice that ever made it into our food was red chili flakes in the broccoli rabe, and even that was rare. I learned to cook with spices as I was exposed to more cuisines and my palate evolved. If you're unsure how to make the most of your spice cabinet, this book will give you some delicious opportunities. If you've had that canister of fennel seeds for a few years, please replace it—spices don't live forever. A small mortar and pestle is a worthwhile purchase so you'll be able to grind some of the whole seeds at a moment's notice.

Allspice

Contrary to some people's belief, this is not a mix of all the spices. It's an aromatic spice that adds a clove-like flavor to dishes. I like it best in meats, especially lamb.

Black Pepper

Freshly ground is the only way to go here. That sad-looking gray dust in the tin can has zero flavor.

Cardamom

Cooking with cardamom is like traveling in your own kitchen—it evokes the vibes of an exotic, faraway land. It's the predominant flavor in chai tea and is an amazing addition to oatmeal.

Cinnamon

One of the most loved spices by all, cinnamon has a beautiful exotic and sweet flavor. Many people use it in sweet dishes, but I hope this book will have you using it in savory recipes, if you don't already.

Cumin Seeds

You'll notice ground cumin is not included in this book. The seeds have so much more flavor and a quick whirl in the mortar and pestle brings it out while breaking down the seeds.

Dried Thyme

Any recipe that calls for dried thyme will also work well if you use fresh. But since fresh thyme is sold only by the bunch, and most recipes use only a few tablespoons of leaves, dried is often the best choice.

Fennel Seeds

These appear throughout the book. They add great flavor that has a slightly sweet anise aroma. Grinding them, even coarsely, avoids the unpleasant bite into a whole seed.

Red Chili Flakes

This is a great source of heat. Don't be afraid to investigate different kinds; Korean, Aleppo, and Kashmiri are all spicy and fragrant in different ways.

Salt

The elemental seasoning for all types of food, its importance cannot be emphasized enough. Throughout the book, I call for kosher salt, but sea salt is also a great substitute. I never, I repeat, never want you to use iodized table salt. There's no place for that stuff in your life. It's highly processed, has a metallic flavor, and the extremely fine grains are hard to control . . . do I need to go on? Big flaky sea salts are a great option for sprinkling on top of dishes just before serving. If no measurement is provided for salt, use your intuition and taste along the way— doing this will help you train your taste buds and hone your cooking skills.

Sugars and Other Sweeteners

I wouldn't advise consuming a large amount of sugar daily, but you'll find small amounts of various kinds of sugar used throughout the book. I use everything from white sugar, to brown sugar, and even coconut palm sugar, but all in moderate quantities. A sweetener I use more liberally is pure maple syrup, and I recommend substituting it for granulated types of sugar wherever possible. When buying maple syrup, it's crucial to buy one where the only ingredient listed on the label is "pure maple syrup."

Sumac

If you've ever had Middle Eastern or Mediterranean food, you might have tasted sumac. It's a dried and ground berry that lends a tart and slightly sweet flavor to salads and meats. It also has a beautiful plum hue that adds great color when it's dusted on a dish.

Turmeric

This electrically colored spice adds a very warm flavor to any dish, especially soups and stews. Not to mention its widely regarded health benefits (strong anti-inflammatory properties, among others). Just be careful because it will stain white clothing, dish towels, and your hands (temporarily).

✳ Seeds and Nuts ✳

Seeds and nuts are great healthy additions to your lunch that add that satisfying crunch factor. If you don't think you'll use them all right away, store them in a cool, dark place or even in the refrigerator.

Almonds, Cashews, Peanuts, Walnuts

Chop them, grind them, eat them whole. These nuts are all delicious on salads, and they're a great source of protein and good fats.

Chia Seeds

Available at most big grocers, chia seeds are tiny nutrient powerhouses. They're loaded with fiber, protein, omega-3 fatty acids, and antioxidants. They also expand in liquid, so they're useful as a natural thickening agent.

Ground Flax Seeds

When flax seeds are left whole, our body can't digest them and they just pass through us. In order to absorb all the amazing benefits of these seeds, they have to be ground.

Hemp Seeds

Relatively new to most supermarkets, these are tiny, nutty seeds that are jam-packed with protein, fiber, and omega-3 fatty acids. Sprinkle them on salads, oatmeal, grain bowls, and almost anything else.

Pepitas

Pepitas are the green inner seed of certain pumpkins. To bring out their flavor, lightly toast them in a dry pan. They're packed with vitamin E, which is great for your skin and hair.

Pine Nuts

Also known as pignoli nuts, they're what give pesto its distinct flavor. Lightly toast them in a dry pan for a nutty, creamy garnish to just about anything. They tend to be expensive, due to how they're harvested, but a little goes a long way, and you can store them in the freezer to extend their shelf life even further.

Sesame Seeds

Both white and black sesame seeds are at their best when they're lightly toasted.

In the Refrigerator

Keep these items in your refrigerator at all times. They don't expire quickly, and they're building blocks of great lunches.

Anchovies

Yeah, yeah. You don't like anchovies. But you love Caesar salad, right? Trust me on this one: Anchovies are your friend. They add depth and saltiness to dressings and sauces. I like buying a tube of anchovy paste for the ease of it, but tinned anchovies are great too. You can transfer what you don't use right away to a jar.

Curry Pastes

Red or green curry pastes can be the inspiration for a whole meal. They are a great refrigerator staple that make whipping up an amazing vegetable curry so easy.

Fresh Herbs

Herbs can elevate just about anything you're making with their distinct flavors and aromas, which is why I use them so often. To properly preserve them, rinse them, dry them well, and store them in a plastic bag with a paper towel for absorbing any excess moisture. If you're not thrilled about storing in plastic, put them in a large glass storage container or a jar lined with a paper towel (trim the stems to make them fit).

Garlic

A few years ago, I made the switch to pre-peeled garlic cloves and I never looked back. It might be more expensive, but not having to clean and peel the garlic while cooking is well worth it. If you're planning on following my lead, they will last you over a month in the refrigerator. If buying a bulb of garlic, however, store it in a dark place, like a pantry, to maximize its shelf life.

Ginger

An unsung hero of the produce section, ginger has a spicy flavor that marries perfectly with garlic or onion flavors in savory dishes. Because it's a root and can be quite fibrous, I like to use a microplane to grate it. You can peel its thin brown skin by simply cutting it off with a sharp knife or scraping it off with a spoon. Those peelings are a great addition to Easy Homemade Chicken Stock (page 18).

Hot Sauce

Lots of dishes benefit from a good dash of hot sauce. Keep it in your refrigerator at home, or in the office. It's good to have on hand.

Lemons and Limes

These citrus fruits are used in many recipes throughout the book, so I advise always having them on hand. Keep them in the crisper drawer and they'll last longer.

Mayonnaise

Sometimes there is nothing else that will do other than a small amount of mayo. Traditional mayos are made with vegetable or soybean oils which are highly processed and unhealthy. Luckily, there are brands that are putting out great mayos with better fats like avocado oil and grapeseed oil. Look for these kinds of mayos and use them whenever your dish needs a bit of creaminess.

Miso

Most commonly made from fermented soybeans, miso is one of nature's greatest gifts. Plus, it will last in your refrigerator for many months and it makes so many dishes infinitely better. If you're just starting on your miso journey, try the milder yellow or white misos first. Red miso is stronger and saltier. Read the ingredients, and look for miso that doesn't contain MSG.

Mustard

For the recipes in this book, grainy or whole-grain mustards are the way to go. They add zip and texture to dressings.

Unsalted Butter

Real cooks use unsalted butter for cooking because it allows them to better control the amount of salt in a dish. (Welcome to the club!) Butter gets a bad rap, but if you're buying organic (and ideally pasture-raised), I believe this is a good fat—and good fats give us energy.

Yogurt

If you're only eating yogurt topped with granola and fruit in the morning, this book will have you using it in new ways. I love the richness it adds to sauces, dressings, and as a topping for savory dishes. I recommend using full-fat Greek yogurt, but you can substitute plain yogurt if you prefer. Yogurt has a ton of probiotics which keep our gut healthy and happy.

Easy Homemade Chicken Stock

If homemade chicken stock had a public relations manager, it would be me; I sing its praises all over town. When you eat something as simple as a grain or rice at a great restaurant and wonder why such a seemingly simple thing is so damn delicious, the answer is probably homemade chicken stock. Although boxed or canned chicken stock, even organic, is very convenient, it also has problems: its flavor varies unpredictably from brand to brand; it's often packed with unnecessary salt that could throw your dish off; it's devoid of any nutritional value; and it's highly processed and contains all sorts of ingredients that you can't pronounce let alone identify.

Here's my pitch: Homemade stock is super simple to make, it's nutritious, it can be used in many ways, and you can store it in pre-portioned amounts in the freezer. To get the bones for the stock, buy a whole bird or ask the butcher to sell you just bones and wings. With the whole bird, you can cut off all the meat to cook separately, then use the carcass for stock. You can also roast the bird, eat the meat, and use the leftover carcass to make the stock. Try swapping out half the amount of water with stock when you cook rice or grains, unless those grains are headed for a sweet dish like Farro Porridge with Yogurt and Caramelized Apples (page 77).

Any amount of chicken bones, wings, and backs

1 onion, quartered

A few garlic cloves

1 to 2 large carrots

1 to 2 celery ribs (optional)

Leftover parsley stems (optional)

3 to 4 peppercorns (optional)

Place all the ingredients in a large pot and add enough water to cover the contents. Bring to a boil, then simmer for anywhere from 3 to 8 hours. Pour the stock through a fine-mesh strainer, divide it into containers, and store in the refrigerator for a week, or in the freezer for 2 to 3 months.

tip

Use your intuition when deciding on the amount of vegetables to add to your stock. You don't want the vegetables to overpower the chicken flavor. So if you have a smaller amount of bones, stick with a smaller amount of vegetables, and vice versa.

Helpful Tools

A Fine-Mesh Strainer

These are great for draining rice, grains, and beans. The small holes ensure your rice won't slip through. They're available in a variety sizes that are not as cumbersome as a colander. If you look online you can find very inexpensive ones that do the job perfectly.

A Mandoline

Sometimes, the way a vegetable is cut is what makes it so appealing. In certain dishes, you really want a julienned carrot instead of a diced one. The easiest way is with a mandoline—it cuts your prep time in half. My favorite brand is Benriner because it's inexpensive, very low tech, and doesn't take up a lot of room. You can find a variety of great mandolines on Amazon.

A Microplane or Rasp

You'll quickly realize I don't let the zest of limes or lemons go to waste. I put zest into lots of dishes. The only way to easily retrieve the fine skin of citrus is with a microplane or rasp. These tools are also great for grating garlic, ginger, and cheese.

A Sharp Knife

This is the numero uno important, take-to-a-desert-island kind of tool. Not only is a dull knife dangerous, but it also makes whatever you're cutting take twice as long.

Immersion Blender or Blender

Although I like low-tech cooking, sometimes the goal is that super smooth texture that's hard to achieve any other way. Both appliances work, and immersion blenders are great for smaller quantities, like those you'll find in this book.

At Your Desk

You never know when your lunch is going to need a bit of sprucing up, so trick out your work desk or any other area where you often find yourself during lunchtime with a little condiment stash. Here are some clever things to keep in your desk or in your office refrigerator:

- Hot sauce
- Mini container of flaky sea salt
- Mini bottle of extra virgin olive oil
- A few soy sauce packets
- Precut lemon wedges
- Precut lime wedges

This Week's Menu

Monday	RICE NOODLE SALAD
Tuesday	COCONUT CURRY NOODLE SOUP
Wednesday	RICE AND LENTIL BOWL WITH CHICKEN MEATBALLS
Thursday	RICE AND LENTIL BOWL WITH ROASTED VEGETABLES
Friday	RED CURRY SHRIMP STIR-FRY

This week delivers an umami bang! Super flavorful chicken meatballs find their way into a satisfying cold noodle salad on Monday, a curry soup on Tuesday, and a lentil bowl on Wednesday. The best part? They come together in a snap and are delicious at any temperature. Lime, fish sauce, and peanuts are dominant flavors this week, and they'll make you forget all about your favorite Vietnamese takeout restaurant. The raw veggies will provide a hit of vitamin C and freshness throughout the week, while the Rice and Lentils in Coconut Milk is a warming, fiber-filled base (not to mention vegan!) that will provide some balance. Store the rice and lentils in the refrigerator right in the pot you cooked them in, which will make reheating a breeze. Throughout the week, add a garnish of torn up cilantro and mint leaves to your bowls; the herbs pack a flavor punch and get you closer to your goal of zero waste at the end of the week.

Grocery List

Make sure you have the following ingredients for the week.

Pantry

8 ounces thin rice noodles

½ cup brown rice

¾ cup red lentils

½ cup panko bread crumbs

Grapeseed oil

5 teaspoons rice wine vinegar

½ teaspoon toasted sesame oil

3 tablespoons fish sauce

4 teaspoons soy sauce

3 teaspoons red curry paste

1 (14-ounce) can full-fat coconut milk

1 (5.4-ounce) can coconut cream

1 teaspoon fennel seeds

1 teaspoon cumin seeds

¼ teaspoon cinnamon

2 teaspoons turmeric

2 teaspoons brown sugar or coconut palm
   sugar

2 cups chicken stock (ideally homemade,
   (see page 18) or water

½ cup roasted salted peanuts

2 tablespoons hemp seeds

Produce

2 garlic cloves

1 (3-inch) piece fresh ginger

2 medium sweet potatoes

2 limes

2 jalapeños

1 small onion

1 large bunch of mint

1 bunch of cilantro

1 bunch of scallions

2 carrots

3 Persian cucumbers

1 bunch (about 5 stems) broccolini

¼ pound shiitake mushrooms

Dairy

1 egg

Meat and Seafood

½ pound ground chicken

¼ pound shrimp (about 6 pieces)—peeled,
   deveined, and frozen until ready to use

Sunday Prep

Make the following recipes:

1 Lime Vinaigrette (see opposite)

2 Ginger Chicken Meatballs (page 26)

3 Rice and Lentils in Coconut Milk (page 28)

4 Spicy Roasted Sweet Potatoes (page 30)

5 Roasted Broccolini (page 31) WED

Prepare and store in sealable containers in the refrigerator:

- Rice noodles: In a large bowl, cover 8 ounces of rice noodles with boiling water. Using tongs, agitate the noodles a little. Let the noodles sit for 20 minutes, or until they are tender. Drain the noodles, rinse them with cold water, and toss with a drizzle of grapeseed oil to prevent sticking. Makes 5 cups of noodles.

- Coconut curry soup base: Mix 1 (5.4-ounce) can coconut cream, 2 teaspoons of red curry paste, 2 teaspoons of fish sauce, 1 teaspoon of soy sauce, ½ teaspoon of grated ginger, and the zest and juice of ½ lime in a small bowl until well combined. Makes 1 serving.

- Chop all the peanuts.

Lime Vinaigrette

☼ Makes ½ cup ☼

¼ cup grapeseed oil

2 tablespoons fish sauce

1 tablespoon rice wine vinegar

2 teaspoons brown sugar or coconut palm sugar

Zest and juice of 1 lime

½ jalapeño, thinly sliced (more if you want a spicy vinaigrette)

Combine all the ingredients in a jar and secure with the lid.

Shake vigorously until the sugar has dissolved.

Store in the refrigerator until ready to use.

Ginger Chicken Meatballs

☼ Makes 8 meatballs ☼

1 tablespoon grapeseed oil

½ pound ground chicken

½ cup panko breadcrumbs

1 egg

1 teaspoon soy sauce

½ teaspoon toasted sesame oil

1 garlic clove, grated or minced

1 (1-inch) piece fresh ginger, peeled and grated or minced

½ bunch mint, finely chopped

½ bunch cilantro, finely chopped

½ teaspoon kosher salt

Heat the oven to 425°F. Line a rimmed baking sheet with parchment paper, brush the paper with 1½ teaspoons of grapeseed oil, and set aside.

Combine the chicken, breadcrumbs, egg, soy sauce, sesame oil, garlic, ginger, mint, cilantro, and salt in a large bowl. Using clean hands, mix everything together until evenly blended. Using your hands, form the mixture into eight 1½-inch balls and place them, evenly spaced, on the prepared baking sheet.

Drizzle the meatballs with the remaining 1½ teaspoons of grapeseed oil and place in the oven. Bake for 12 to16 minutes until an instant-read thermometer placed in the center of the meatballs reads at least 165°F.

Remove from the oven and let cool before storing in an airtight container in the refrigerator.

Rice and Lentils in Coconut Milk

✿ Makes 4 cups ✿

1 tablespoon grapeseed oil

1 small onion, finely chopped

1 teaspoon fennel seeds, lightly ground

1 teaspoon cumin seeds, lightly ground

½ cup brown rice

¼ teaspoon cinnamon

2 teaspoons turmeric

1 teaspoon kosher salt

1 (14-ounce) can full-fat coconut milk

2 cups chicken stock or water

¾ cup red lentils

Heat the oil in a Dutch oven or a heavy-bottomed pan over medium heat. Sauté the onion for 3 minutes until it has softened. Add the fennel seeds, cumin seeds, rice, cinnamon, turmeric, and salt, and stir to combine. Cook for 1 more minute.

Pour in the coconut milk and stock. Bring the mixture to a boil, then cover and reduce to a simmer. Cook for 35 minutes, stirring occasionally.

Add the lentils and simmer with the lid off for another 15 minutes, or until the texture is thick and creamy. If there's still a lot of liquid after 15 minutes, simmer for a few more minutes. Store in an airtight container in the refrigerator.

Spicy Roasted Sweet Potatoes

✿ Makes about 2 cups ✿

---

2 medium sweet potatoes, cut into 1-inch cubes

2 teaspoons rice wine vinegar

1 tablespoon grapeseed oil

¾ teaspoon kosher salt

½ jalapeño, sliced

Heat the oven to 375°F. Toss all the ingredients together in a large bowl and mix until combined.

Lay everything out in an even layer on a rimmed baking sheet and place in the oven. Roast for 25 to 30 minutes, tossing halfway through, until the sweet potatoes are browned on the outside and tender when pierced with a fork. Store in an airtight container in the refrigerator.

Roasted Broccolini

✿ Makes 1½ cups ✿

1 bunch broccolini (about 5 stems)

2 teaspoons grapeseed oil

½ teaspoon soy sauce

1 teaspoon fish sauce

Heat the oven to 425°F. Place the broccolini on a rimmed baking sheet. Drizzle with the oil, soy sauce, and fish sauce. Toss to combine and place in the oven.

Roast for 15 to 20 minutes until tender and crispy in places. Store in an airtight container in the refrigerator.

Rice Noodle Salad

2 cups cooked rice noodles

3 Ginger Chicken Meatballs (page 26)

1 carrot, cut into thin strips

2 Persian cucumbers, cut into thin strips

2 tablespoons Lime Vinaigrette (page 25)

2 tablespoons chopped peanuts

Torn mint leaves

Torn cilantro leaves

¼ jalapeño, thinly sliced

Make a bed of the cooked rice noodles in the bottom of the bowl.

Top with the meatballs, carrots, and cucumbers, then drizzle with the vinaigrette.

Top with the peanuts, mint, cilantro, and jalapeño.

☼ **Tip** ☼ The best technique for making long, thin strips from your vegetables is by using the shredding attachment on a mandoline. It will create uniform strips that mimic the shape and texture of the rice noodles and maximize the flavor combos. Alternatively, you can slice the vegetables thinly with a sharp knife.

Coconut Curry Noodle Soup

1 serving coconut curry soup base

2 cups cooked rice noodles

3 to 4 shiitake mushrooms, thinly sliced

2 Ginger Chicken Meatballs (page 26)

¾ cup Spicy Roasted Sweet Potatoes (page 30)

2 scallions, thinly sliced

Torn mint leaves

Torn cilantro leaves

¼ jalapeño, thinly sliced

Place the coconut curry soup base in the bottom of a bowl.

Top with the rice noodles, mushrooms, meatballs, sweet potatoes, scallions, mint, cilantro, and jalapeño slices.

Right before you're ready to eat, add enough boiling water to the soup to cover all the ingredients, about 2 cups.

Rice and Lentil Bowl
with Chicken Meatballs

2 cups Rice and Lentils in Coconut Milk (page 28)

3 Ginger Chicken Meatballs (page 26)

1 Persian cucumber, thinly sliced

½ cup Spicy Roasted Sweet Potatoes (page 30)

2 tablespoons Lime Vinaigrette (page 25)

Hemp seeds

Torn cilantro leaves

Place the rice and lentils in the bottom of a bowl.

Top with the meatballs, cucumber, and sweet potatoes.

Drizzle the vinaigrette over the cucumber and sprinkle with the hemp seeds and cilantro.

Rice and Lentil Bowl
with Roasted Vegetables

2 cups Rice and Lentils in Coconut Milk (page 28)

1 cup Roasted Broccolini (page 31)

½ cup Spicy Roasted Sweet Potatoes (page 30)

1 scallion, thinly sliced

1 tablespoon Lime Vinaigrette (page 25)

2 tablespoons chopped peanuts

Torn mint leaves

Place the rice and lentils in the bottom of a bowl.

Top with the broccolini, sweet potatoes, and scallion.

Drizzle the vinaigrette over the vegetables and sprinkle with chopped peanuts and mint.

Red Curry Shrimp Stir-Fry

1 teaspoon red curry paste

1 teaspoon soy sauce

2 tablespoons grapeseed oil

1 garlic clove, sliced

1 (1-inch) piece fresh ginger, peeled and minced

¼ jalapeño, thinly sliced

¼ pound shrimp (about 6 pieces), defrosted if frozen

1 carrot, peeled and thinly sliced

Any remaining Roasted Broccolini (page 31), cut into bite-size pieces

Any remaining shiitake mushrooms, sliced (about ¼ cup)

1 tablespoon Lime Vinaigrette (page 25)

1 scallion, cut into 2-inch-long pieces

1 cup cooked rice noodles

1 tablespoon chopped peanuts

Torn cilantro leaves

In a small bowl, mix 2 tablespoons of water with the curry paste and soy sauce until well combined. Set aside.

Heat the oil, garlic, ginger, and jalapeño in a large skillet over medium high heat. Cook, stirring often, for 1 minute, or until the garlic and ginger have softened. Add the shrimp and cook for 3 minutes, tossing often. Using tongs, remove the shrimp from the skillet and set aside.

Cook the carrot, broccolini, and mushrooms in the same skillet, stirring often, for another minute. Add the curry sauce and cook for 2 minutes until the vegetables are tender and some of the liquid has evaporated. Drizzle in the vinaigrette, then stir in the scallion and shrimp.

Place the rice noodles in the bottom of a bowl.

Top with the stir-fry, peanuts, and cilantro.

This Week's Menu

Monday QUINOA BOWL WITH HALLOUMI AND CARROT SLAW

Tuesday QUINOA BOWL WITH A 6-MINUTE EGG

Wednesday HALLOUMI ARUGULA SALAD WITH PICKLED BEETS AND CUCUMBERS

Thursday QUINOA SALAD NIÇOISE

Friday PASTA WITH TUNA AND ARUGULA

All the health buzzwords and advice that's out there can sometimes be overwhelming noise. One simple rule of thumb is that the more colors you have on your plate, the more likely it is to be nutritionally well-rounded. This week brings all the hues to your lunches: beet purple, carrot orange, and parsley and arugula green, while the protein comes in the form of crispy, salty halloumi cheese and oil-packed tuna. Halloumi hails from Cyprus, where it's usually quickly griddled in a hot pan to create a beautiful golden crust. Leave the small task of frying the halloumi until the morning right before you pack your bowl up. As for tuna, look for one that's packed in olive oil in a glass jar— this kind of tuna is the much more refined, flavorful cousin to the tuna packed in water you might be used to, and it's worthy of being front and center in a salad.

Grocery List

Make sure you have the following ingredients for the week.

Pantry

1 ½ cups quinoa

½ teaspoon cumin seeds

2 tablespoons apple cider vinegar

5 tablespoons white wine vinegar

Canola oil

Grapeseed oil

Extra virgin olive oil

¾ cup (about 18) pitted kalamata olives

4 ounces (1-inch bundle) spaghetti

1 (7-ounce) jar olive oil–packed tuna

½ teaspoon anchovy paste

Flaky sea salt

Produce

3 medium beets

3 large carrots or 2 cups shredded carrots

1 bunch parsley

3 Persian cucumbers

2 lemons

3 garlic cloves

1 bunch scallions

1 small shallot

1 (5-ounce) container baby arugula, or
  2 bunches

1 pint cherry tomatoes

When storing greens in plastic containers, open the container and place a sheet of paper towel on top of the greens, then close the lid and store upside down. The paper towel in the bottom absorbs any liquid and keeps your greens fresh longer.

Dairy

2 eggs

1 (8-ounce) package halloumi cheese (or any kind of grilling cheese)

Sunday Prep

Make the following recipes:

1 Simple Roasted Beets (see opposite)

2 Moroccan Carrot Slaw (page 46)

3 Beet-Stained Quinoa (page 48)

4 Pickled Beets and Cucumbers (page 48)

Prepare and store in sealable containers in the refrigerator:

● Quinoa: In a medium saucepan, bring 3 cups salted water to a boil. Add 1½ cups of quinoa, reduce to a simmer, and cook covered for 15 minutes, or until the water has evaporated. Turn off the heat, fluff the quinoa with a fork, cover, and let steam for 5 minutes. Makes about 4½ cups of cooked quinoa.

● 6-minute eggs: Bring a small saucepan of water to a boil. Using a spoon, carefully add 2 eggs. Reduce the heat to a gentle boil and cook for 6 minutes. Rinse with cold water before storing.

● Unwrap and slice the halloumi into ¼-inch pieces. Pat dry with paper towels.

Simple Roasted Beets

3 medium beets

Heat the oven to 350°F.

Trim the tops and ends of each beet and rinse it under running water. Without drying the beets off, wrap each one in a separate square of aluminum foil. Place all the beets on a baking sheet and bake for about 35 to 60 minutes (depending on the size of the beets), turning them halfway through. The beets are done when a fork or paring knife slides easily to the center of the beet.

Remove the beets from the oven, unwrap them, and set aside until cool enough to handle. Alternatively, you can run the whole beet under cold water to speed things up. Using your hands, rub the skins off the beets. Store in an airtight container in the refrigerator.

Moroccan Carrot Slaw

✿ Makes 2 cups ✿

3 large carrots, peeled and ends trimmed (or 2 cups shredded carrots)

2 tablespoons olive oil

2 garlic cloves, minced

½ teaspoon cumin seeds, ground

½ teaspoon kosher salt

Juice of ½ lemon

1 small handful parsley, finely chopped

Cut each carrot in half crosswise. Using a mandoline with a julienne attachment, julienne the carrots. Alternatively, using a knife, cut the carrots into matchsticks.

Heat the oil in a large skillet over medium heat and add the garlic. Cook the garlic, stirring often, for 2 minutes, or until fragrant and soft but not browned. Stir in the cumin seeds and add the carrots and salt. Toss using a pair of tongs. Cook the carrots, tossing often, for 2 to 3 minutes until they are slightly softened but still crunchy.

Turn off the heat, add the lemon juice and parsley, and toss to combine. Store in an airtight container in the refrigerator.

Beet-Stained Quinoa

☼ Makes 3 cups ☼

---

2 ½ cups cooked quinoa

2 Simple Roasted Beets (page 45), cut into small cubes

3 scallions, sliced

2 tablespoons apple cider vinegar

2 tablespoons extra virgin olive oil

Zest of 1 lemon

1 small handful parsley, finely chopped

Kosher salt

In a large bowl, stir together the quinoa, beets, scallions, vinegar, oil, lemon zest, and parsley. Add salt to taste.

Store in an airtight container in the refrigerator.

Pickled Beets and Cucumbers

☼ Makes 1 cup ☼

---

1 Simple Roasted Beet (page 45), cut into medium cubes

1 Persian cucumber, diced

1 shallot, very thinly sliced

3 tablespoons white wine vinegar

2 tablespoons olive oil

Juice of ½ lemon

½ teaspoon kosher salt

Place all the ingredients in a bowl and toss well to combine.

Transfer to a jar or an airtight container and store in the refrigerator.

Quinoa Bowl with Halloumi and Carrot Slaw

1 tablespoon grapeseed oil

3 slices halloumi cheese

1 cup arugula

1½ cups Beet-Stained Quinoa (page 48)

1 cup Moroccan Carrot Slaw (page 46)

¼ cup (about 6) kalamata olives

Heat the oil in a small nonstick skillet over medium heat. Pat the halloumi slices dry with a paper towel and place in the pan (if your halloumi is wet, you won't get the crispy crust). Cook for 1 to 2 minutes on each side until a golden-brown crust forms. Transfer to a plate and set aside.

Place the arugula, quinoa, and carrot slaw in a bowl in three separate sections, then top with the halloumi slices and olives.

Quinoa Bowl with a 6-Minute Egg

1½ cups Beet-Stained Quinoa (page 48)

½ cup arugula

½ cup cherry tomatoes, halved

1 Persian cucumber, diced

One 6-minute minute egg, peeled and halved

1 tablespoon extra virgin olive oil

Flaky sea salt

Torn parsley leaves

Place the quinoa in the bottom of a bowl.

Top with the arugula, tomatoes, cucumber, and egg.

Drizzle with the oil, then sprinkle with salt and parsley.

Halloumi Arugula Salad
with Pickled Beets and Cucumbers

1 tablespoon grapeseed oil

3 slices halloumi cheese

1½ cups arugula

1 cup Moroccan Carrot Slaw (page 46)

1 cup Pickled Beets and Cucumbers (page 48)

Heat the oil in a small nonstick skillet over medium heat. Pat the halloumi dry with a paper towel and place in the pan (if your halloumi is wet, you won't get the crispy crust). Cook for 1 to 2 minutes on each side until a golden-brown crust forms. Transfer to a plate and set aside.

Place the arugula, carrot slaw, and pickled vegetables in a bowl in three separate sections, then top with the halloumi slices.

Quinoa Salad Niçoise

1½ cups cooked quinoa

1 cup arugula

1 Persian cucumber, diced

2 tablespoons extra virgin olive oil

2 tablespoons white wine vinegar

½ (7-ounce) jar olive oil–packed tuna, drained

¼ cup (about 6) pitted kalamata olives

One 6-minute egg, peeled and halved

Flaky sea salt

Torn parsley leaves

Place the quinoa, arugula, and cucumber in the bowl. Drizzle with the oil and vinegar.

Using a fork, flake the tuna on top of the salad.

Top with the olives and egg, then sprinkle with salt and parsley.

Pasta with Tuna and Arugula

Kosher salt

4 ounces (1-inch bundle) spaghetti

2 tablespoons olive oil

1 garlic clove, minced

½ teaspoon anchovy paste

1 ½ cups cherry tomatoes, halved

½ (7-ounce) jar olive oil–packed tuna, drained

¼ cup (about 6) pitted kalamata olives

½ cup arugula

1 small handful parsley, chopped

Black pepper

Bring a medium pot of salted water to a boil. Add the pasta and cook according to the package directions until al dente. Drain and set aside.

While the pasta is cooking, heat the oil in a medium skillet over medium heat. Add the garlic, anchovy paste, and tomatoes. Sauté for 5 minutes, stirring often, until the garlic is fragrant and the tomatoes start to break down and release their juices, creating a sauce.

Using a fork, flake the tuna and add it to the skillet along with the olives and arugula. Cook for 1 more minute. Turn off the heat and stir in the pasta and parsley.

Place everything in a bowl and garnish with a sprinkling of salt and pepper.

tip

If you have any bits of halloumi left over, crisp them up in a pan then tear into pieces and toss on top of the pasta. Although some people scoff at the idea of fish and cheese together (99.9% of Italians), in this instance it is delicious and highly acceptable.

This Week's Menu

Monday	FARRO BOWL WITH CHICKEN SKEWERS
Tuesday	KALE AND BRUSSELS SPROUTS SLAW SALAD
Wednesday	FARRO AND VEGETABLE BOWL
Thursday	SAUSAGE AND BUTTERNUT SQUASH PASTA
Friday	FARRO PORRIDGE WITH YOGURT AND CARAMELIZED APPLES

This week brings the flavors of squash, sage, and apples to your lunch bowl. A big batch of roasted squash carries you through the week as it's paired with Yogurt-Marinated Chicken Skewers and later pureed into a silky pasta sauce. Dusting your bowls with the Seed Sprinkle will not only add a salty crunch to any dish, but also provide nutrition (think all the good oils and antioxidants from pepitas, flax seeds, and chia seeds). Farro creates a hearty base for many of the bowls before it's transformed into a lightly sweetened porridge on Friday. A few shavings of Parmigiano-Reggiano can take your lunch to that next salty, satisfying level. Spend a little more money on Parmigiano imported from Italy, which is rich and complex, rather than domestic Parmesan, which lacks some of the flavor and texture. It's a worthwhile investment.

Grocery List

Make sure you have the following ingredients for the week.

Pantry

1½ cups farro
¾ cup rolled oats
2 cups penne or mezzi rigatoni
Extra virgin olive oil
Grapeseed oil
4 teaspoons apple cider vinegar
½ teaspoon soy sauce
3 tablespoons pure maple syrup
2 teaspoons chia seeds
3 tablespoons ground flax seeds
½ cup pepitas
½ teaspoon cumin seeds
½ teaspoon cayenne
1 teaspoon caraway seeds
1 teaspoon cinnamon
1 cup chicken stock (ideally homemade, see page 18) or water
1 tablespoon brown sugar or coconut palm sugar

Produce

7 garlic cloves
1 lemon
1 bunch cilantro
1 bunch mint
1 small bunch sage
1 (1-inch) piece fresh ginger
1 (1½-pound) butternut squash (or the equivalent in precut squash)
1 Fuji or Gala apple
1 bunch lacinato kale (about 10 stems)
½ pound Brussels sprouts or 4 cups shredded Brussels sprouts
1 (5-ounce) container baby arugula, or 2 bunches

Dairy

1 egg
2 tablespoons butter
1¼ cups full-fat Greek yogurt
1 small block Parmigiano-Reggiano
1½ cups unsweetened almond milk

Meat

¼ pound (1 link) sweet Italian sausage
1 pound boneless, skinless chicken thighs

Spend a little less and buy skin-on and bone-in chicken thighs. Remove and render the skin (for technique see page 122) and cut out the bones, then use them to make chicken stock.

Special Equipment

5 (6-inch) metal or wooden skewers

Sunday Prep

Make the following recipes:

1 Cilantro and Mint Chutney (see opposite)

2 Kale and Brussels Sprouts Slaw (page 65)

3 Yogurt-Marinated Chicken Skewers (page 66)

4 Roasted Butternut Squash with Sage (page 67)

5 Seed Sprinkle (page 69)

Prepare and store in sealable containers in the refrigerator:

● Farro: Bring a medium saucepan of salted water to a boil. Add 1½ cups of farro and continue to boil for 25 to 30 minutes until the farro is tender but still slightly chewy. Drain the farro and rinse it with cold water. Makes about 3 cups of cooked farro.

● 7-minute egg: Bring a small saucepan of water to a boil. Using a spoon, carefully add the egg. Reduce the heat to a gentle boil and cook for 7 minutes. Rinse with cold water before storing.

Cilantro and Mint Chutney

☼ Makes ½ cup ☼

1 cup cilantro leaves

½ cup mint leaves

½ cup full-fat Greek yogurt

1 garlic clove

1 (1-inch) piece fresh ginger, peeled

¼ teaspoon kosher salt, plus more to taste

¼ teaspoon cumin seeds

⅛ teaspoon cayenne (optional)

Combine all the ingredients in a blender and blend until very smooth. Season with more salt to taste.

Transfer to a jar and store in the refrigerator.

Kale and Brussels Sprouts Slaw

☼ Makes about 4½ cups ☼

1 garlic clove, grated or minced

1 tablespoon extra virgin olive oil

1 tablespoon apple cider vinegar

½ teaspoon kosher salt

½ pound Brussels sprouts, trimmed, or 4 cups shredded Brussels sprouts

½ bunch lacinato kale, ribs removed

1 teaspoon caraway seeds

¼ cup freshly grated Parmigiano-Reggiano

Black pepper

In a large bowl, combine the garlic, oil, vinegar, and salt. Whisk to combine and set aside.

Using a mandoline or sharp knife, thinly slice all the Brussels sprouts. (Skip this step if using shredded Brussels sprouts.) Stack the kale leaves on top of each other, roll them up like a cigar, and slice crosswise into thin ribbons. Transfer both vegetables to the bowl.

Top the slaw with the caraway seeds, cheese, and a few grinds of black pepper, then toss to combine. Store in an airtight container in the refrigerator.

Yogurt-Marinated Chicken Skewers

☼ Makes 4 to 5 skewers ☼

½ cup full-fat Greek yogurt

3 garlic cloves, smashed

Zest of ½ lemon

1½ teaspoons kosher salt

½ teaspoon cinnamon

¼ teaspoon cayenne

¼ teaspoon cumin seeds, coarsely ground

1 pound boneless, skinless chicken thighs, cut into 1-inch pieces

5 (6-inch) metal or wooden skewers

In a large bowl, combine all the ingredients. Mix well so that the chicken is evenly coated with the marinade. Cover with plastic wrap and let marinate in the refrigerator for at least 1 hour or up to 8 hours.

Before cooking the chicken, soak the wooden skewers in water for 20 minutes. Thread the chicken onto the skewers, packing the pieces tightly together.

Grill method: Heat your grill to high. Grill the chicken for 12 to 15 minutes, turning often, until a nice char develops and an instant-read thermometer inserted into the chicken reads 160°F to 165°F.

Oven method: Place the skewers on a baking sheet. With the oven rack in the upper position, turn the broiler to high. Broil the chicken for 5 to 8 minutes, turning often, until a nice char develops on all sides. Turn off the broiler and turn the oven temperature to 450°F. Bake the chicken for another 8 to 10 minutes until an instant-read thermometer inserted into the chicken reads 160°F to 165°F.

Let the chicken cool before storing in an airtight container in the refrigerator.

Roasted Butternut Squash with Sage

✿ Makes 4 cups ✿

1 (1½-pound) butternut squash

3 tablespoons grapeseed oil

10 whole sage leaves

1 teaspoon kosher salt

Heat the oven to 425°F and place the oven racks in the upper and lower positions.

Peel and cut the squash in half lengthwise. Using a spoon, scrape out and discard the seeds. Cut the squash into 1½-inch pieces. (Skip these steps if using precut squash.)

In a large bowl, combine the squash with the oil, sage, and salt, and toss to combine. Lay the squash out on 2 baking sheets in one even layer (the more room between pieces, the crispier they will be) and place in the oven.

Roast the squash for 30 to 40 minutes, tossing once or twice, and rotating the baking sheets between upper and lower racks halfway through baking, until the squash is tender or lightly browned all over. Let cool before storing in an airtight container in the refrigerator.

Seed Sprinkle

✿ Makes 1 cup ✿

½ cup pepitas

¼ cup rolled oats

2 tablespoons ground flax seeds

2 teaspoons chia seeds

1 tablespoon grapeseed oil

1 tablespoon pure maple syrup

½ teaspoon soy sauce

½ teaspoon kosher salt

⅛ teaspoon cayenne (optional, but delicious)

Heat the oven to 350°F. Line a baking sheet with parchment paper or aluminum foil.

In a medium bowl, combine the pepitas, oats, ground flax seeds, and chia seeds. Add the oil, maple syrup, soy sauce, salt, and cayenne (if using). Stir everything together and place the mixture on the prepared baking sheet in one even layer. Bake for 25 to 35 minutes, stirring once or twice, until everything is toasted and dry.

Store in an airtight container at room temperature.

✿
tip
✿
You won't be sorry if you decide to double this recipe. This seed sprinkle is amazing on everything from yogurt breakfast bowls to salads. Eating it straight out of your hand is also a great choice for an afternoon snack.

Farro Bowl with Chicken Skewers

1 cup cooked farro

1 cup Roasted Butternut Squash with Sage (page 67)

2 cups Kale and Brussels Sprouts Slaw (page 65)

2 Yogurt-Marinated Chicken Skewers (page 66)

¼ cup Cilantro and Mint Chutney (page 63)

Torn mint leaves

Place the farro, squash, and slaw in the bottom of a bowl.

Top with the skewers, drizzle with the chutney, and sprinkle with the mint.

Kale and Brussels Sprouts Slaw Salad

1 teaspoon extra virgin olive oil

½ teaspoon apple cider vinegar

2 cups arugula

2½ cups Kale and Brussels Sprouts Slaw (page 65)

½ apple, thinly sliced

2 or 3 Yogurt-Marinated Chicken Skewers (page 66)

¼ cup Seed Sprinkle (page 69)

A few shavings of Parmigiano-Reggiano

Black pepper

Place the oil and vinegar in the bottom of a bowl.

Top with the arugula, slaw, apple, and chicken skewers.

Garnish the bowl with the seed sprinkle, shaved Parmigiano-Reggiano, and a few grinds of black pepper.

Farro and Vegetable Bowl

2 tablespoons extra virgin olive oil

1 garlic clove, minced

½ bunch lacinato kale, ribs removed and chopped

Kosher salt

1 cup cooked farro

2 cups arugula

½ teaspoon apple cider vinegar

1 cup Roasted Butternut Squash with Sage (page 67)

One 7-minute egg, peeled and halved

¼ cup Cilantro and Mint Chutney (page 63)

A few shavings of Parmigiano-Reggiano

¼ cup Seed Sprinkle (page 69)

Torn cilantro leaves

Torn mint leaves

In a large skillet over medium-high heat, heat 1 tablespoon of oil. When the oil is hot, add the garlic and cook for 1 minute until soft. Add the kale and cook for 2 minutes until wilted. Turn off the heat and season with a pinch of salt.

Place the farro and arugula in the bottom of a bowl and drizzle with the vinegar and remaining 1 tablespoon of oil.

Top with the kale, squash, egg, and chutney.

Garnish with the Parmigiano-Reggiano, seed sprinkle, cilantro, and mint.

Sausage and Butternut Squash Pasta

Kosher salt

2 cups penne or mezzi rigatoni

1 tablespoon grapeseed oil

¼ pound (1 link) sweet Italian sausage, casing removed

1 garlic clove, chopped

3 sage leaves, chopped

1½ cups Roasted Butternut Squash with Sage (page 67)

1 cup chicken stock

¼ cup grated Parmigiano-Reggiano

¼ cup Seed Sprinkle (page 69)

Sliced mint leaves

Bring a medium pot of salted water to a boil. Add the pasta and cook according to the package directions until al dente. Drain and set aside.

In a medium saucepan over medium-high heat, heat the oil. Crumble in the sausage and cook for 3 to 4 minutes, breaking up the sausage with a wooden spoon, until lightly browned and cooked through. Transfer the sausage to a plate, leaving the fat in the pan. Add the garlic and sage and sauté for 1 minute until fragrant.

Add the squash and stock and season with salt, then simmer for 5 minutes. Using an immersion blender, carefully blend the contents of the pan until velvety smooth. If the sauce is too thick, add a little water or stock. You can also do this in a regular blender, but be sure to hold a dish towel over the lid when you blend because the sauce will be hot.

Add the pasta, reserved sausage, and Parmigiano-Reggiano and toss with the sauce. Place the pasta in a bowl and top with the seed sprinkle and mint.

Farro Porridge with Yogurt and Caramelized Apples

1½ cups unsweetened almond milk

½ teaspoon kosher salt

½ teaspoon cinnamon

1 cup cooked farro

½ cup rolled oats

2 tablespoons pure maple syrup

1 tablespoon ground flax seeds

2 tablespoons butter

½ apple, sliced

1 tablespoon brown sugar or coconut palm sugar

¼ cup full-fat Greek yogurt

¼ cup Seed Sprinkle (page 69)

In a medium saucepan over medium heat, heat the almond milk, salt, cinnamon, farro, and oats. Bring the mixture to a simmer and cook for 5 minutes, stirring often. Turn off the heat and stir in the maple syrup and ground flax seeds.

Meanwhile, in a small skillet over medium-high heat, melt the butter. Add the apple slices and sugar and cook for 4 to 5 minutes, or until soft.

Place the porridge in the bottom of a bowl. Top with the yogurt and add the apple. Scatter the seed sprinkle over the porridge.

This Week's Menu

Monday	SOBA NOODLE SALAD WITH MISO SALMON
Tuesday	BLACK RICE BOWL WITH MISO SALMON AND SPINACH
Wednesday	MISO SOBA NOODLE SOUP
Thursday	SPINACH SALAD WITH SUGAR SNAP PEAS AND SOY SAUCE EGGS
Friday	FRIED BLACK RICE

This week is all about miso and soy, some of the most delicious ingredients on the planet. Miso has many more applications than just the miso soup you get with your sushi. This week, you'll be blitzing this flavorful paste into a dressing, rubbing it on salmon, and using it as a base for a noodle soup bowl packed with veggies and soba noodles. If you buy good quality, ideally organic, miso, it will provide you with probiotics and vitamin K. Novice miso shoppers should know that the light shades (white and yellow) are aged less and are therefore milder, best for soups and dressing, while the darker shades (red) have a stronger flavor and are best used in braises and stews. And if you've ever eaten a bowl of ramen noodles, you've probably had an egg similar to the Soy Sauce Jammy Eggs in this chapter. The eggs are cooked for just 6½ minutes before they take a plunge in a soy sauce bath, which creates an egg that is greater than the sum of its parts and so satisfying. Make a few extra for snacks during the week!

Grocery List

Make sure you have the following ingredients for the week.

Pantry

½ cup plus 1 tablespoon white or
    yellow miso paste
½ cup soy sauce
Grapeseed oil
3 tablespoons rice wine vinegar
3 teaspoons toasted sesame oil
9 ounces buckwheat soba noodles
1½ cups black rice
¼ cup sesame seeds
2 tablespoons hemp seeds
½ cup roasted salted cashews
A pinch of red chili flakes (optional)
Chili oil (optional)

Produce

1 (3-inch) piece fresh ginger
3 garlic cloves
1 lemon
3 carrots
2 Persian cucumbers
1 (5-ounce) container baby spinach
1 bunch scallions
½ pound sugar snap peas
½ pound shiitake mushrooms
1 cup any microgreens or sprouts

Seafood

1 (½-pound) salmon fillet

Dairy

4 eggs

Sunday Prep

Make the following recipes:

1 Carrot Miso Dressing (page 84)

2 Salty Cucumbers (page 84)

3 Miso-Marinated Salmon (page 85)

4 Soy Sauce Jammy Eggs (page 86)

Prepare and store in sealable containers in the refrigerator:

● Soba noodles: Bring a medium saucepan of salted water to a boil. Add 9 ounces of soba noodles and cook for 3 minutes, or until just tender. Drain the noodles, rinse with cold water, and toss them with a few drops of grapeseed oil to prevent sticking. Makes 4 cups of noodles.

● Black rice: Bring a medium saucepan of salted water to a boil. Add 1½ cups of black rice. Boil for 30 minutes, then drain and rinse with cold water. Makes 3½ cups of cooked rice.

● Toasted sesame seeds: Place all the sesame seeds in a small, dry skillet and turn the heat up to medium. Toast, shaking often, until the seeds become lightly golden brown.

● Miso soup base: Mix 2 tablespoons of miso paste, 1 teaspoon of grated ginger, 1 small grated garlic clove, and 1 teaspoon of soy sauce with ¼ cup of very hot water. Makes 1 serving.

● Chop all the roasted cashews.

Carrot Miso Dressing

✿ Makes about ½ cup ✿

¼ cup grapeseed oil

3 tablespoons rice wine vinegar

Juice from ½ lemon

1 medium carrot, peeled and chopped

2 tablespoons miso paste

1 (1-inch) piece fresh ginger, peeled and chopped

1 teaspoon toasted sesame oil

1 teaspoon soy sauce

Place all the ingredients in a blender and blend until very smooth. If the consistency is too thick, add water, a tablespoon at a time, until the dressing is pourable.

Store in a covered jar in the refrigerator.

Salty Cucumbers

✿ Makes 1¼ cups ✿

---

2 Persian cucumbers

¼ teaspoon toasted sesame oil

1 garlic clove, smashed

½ teaspoon kosher salt

Pinch of red chili flakes (optional)

Using a mandoline, slice the cucumbers very thinly.

Transfer them to a bowl and toss with the oil, garlic, salt, and chili flakes (if using).

Let the cucumbers sit for 20 minutes, then pour off any liquid that has accumulated in the bottom of the bowl.

Store the cucumbers in an airtight container in the refrigerator.

Miso-Marinated Salmon

☼ Makes 2 servings ☼

1 tablespoon miso paste

1½ teaspoons grapeseed oil

½ teaspoon toasted sesame oil

Zest from ½ lemon

1 (½-pound) salmon fillet

In a small bowl, using a fork, combine the miso paste, grapeseed oil, sesame oil, and lemon zest until a thick paste forms. Using clean hands, rub the paste all over the salmon and transfer it to a plate.

Cover the salmon with plastic wrap and let it marinate in the refrigerator for at least 15 minutes and up to 1 hour.

Turn the oven broiler on high. Place the salmon on a rimmed baking sheet lined with parchment paper or aluminum foil. Broil the salmon for 3 minutes, or until it starts to brown in spots. Turn the broiler off, heat the oven to 475°F and bake for another 5 to 7 minutes, until the salmon flakes easily when pierced with a fork.

Store the salmon in an airtight container in the refrigerator.

Soy Sauce Jammy Eggs

☼ Makes 4 eggs ☼

1 cup hot water

¼ cup soy sauce

1 teaspoon sugar

4 eggs, at room temperature

In a jar or container large enough to fit 4 eggs, combine the water, soy sauce, and sugar. Stir until the sugar has dissolved and set the jar aside.

Bring a small saucepan of water to a boil. Using a spoon, carefully add the eggs. Reduce the heat to a gentle boil and cook for 6½ minutes.

Remove the eggs from the pan and run them under cold water to stop the cooking. When the eggs are cool, peel them and place in the jar with the soy sauce mixture. If there is not enough liquid to cover the eggs, either transfer them to a smaller container or add a little more water and soy sauce.

Let the eggs marinate for at least 1 hour before eating. The flavor will intensify as the eggs sit in their soy sauce bath.

Soba Noodle Salad with Miso Salmon

2 cups cooked soba noodles

1 cup baby spinach

2 tablespoons Carrot Miso Dressing (page 84)

½ cup Salty Cucumbers (page 84)

1 carrot, peeled and cut into ribbons using a peeler

1 scallion, thinly sliced

1 serving Miso-Marinated Salmon (page 85), flaked

Toasted sesame seeds

¼ cup microgreens

Place the noodles and spinach in the bottom of a bowl and drizzle with 1 tablespoon of dressing.

Top with the cucumbers, carrot, and scallion.

Add the salmon on top, drizzle with the remaining tablespoon of dressing, and sprinkle with toasted sesame seeds and microgreens.

Black Rice Bowl with Miso Salmon and Spinach

¼ cup sugar snap peas, thinly sliced

1½ cups cooked black rice

½ cup Salty Cucumbers (page 84)

1 cup baby spinach

1 serving Miso-Marinated Salmon (page 85), flaked

2 tablespoons Carrot Miso Dressing (page 84)

Hemp seeds

Chopped roasted cashews

¼ cup microgreens

Bring a small pot of salted water to a boil. Add the sugar snap peas and cook for 1½ minutes. Drain them immediately and rinse with cold water. Set aside.

Place the rice in the bottom of a bowl.

Top with the sugar snap peas, cucumbers, and spinach. Add the salmon on top, drizzle with the dressing, and garnish with hemp seeds, cashews, and microgreens.

Miso Soba Noodle Soup

1 serving miso soup base

2 cups cooked soba noodles

5 shiitake mushrooms, sliced

1 cup spinach leaves

1 Soy Sauce Jammy Egg (page 86), halved

Toasted sesame seeds

1 scallion, sliced

Chili oil (optional)

Place the miso soup base in the bottom of a bowl.

Top with the noodles, followed by the mushrooms, spinach, and egg. Garnish with the sesame seeds and scallion.

When you're ready to eat, pour enough boiling water (about 2½ cups) into the bowl to cover the noodles and vegetables. Let sit for 1 minute until the spinach is wilted, then gently stir to mix everything tougher.

Drizzle with a few drops of chili oil (if using).

Spinach Salad with Sugar Snap Peas and Soy Sauce Eggs

½ cup sugar snap peas

3 cups baby spinach

1 scallion, sliced

¼ cup Carrot Miso Dressing (page 84)

¼ cup Salty Cucumbers (page 84)

2 Soy Sauce Jammy Eggs (page 86), halved

Chopped roasted cashews

Toasted sesame seeds

¼ cup microgreens

Bring a small pot of salted water to a boil. Add the sugar snap peas and cook for 1 ½ minutes. Drain them immediately and rinse with cold water. Set aside.

Place the spinach, sugar snap peas, and scallion in the bottom of a bowl and drizzle with the dressing.

Top with the cucumbers and eggs.

Garnish with cashews, sesame seeds, and microgreens.

Fried Black Rice

3 tablespoons grapeseed oil

1 garlic clove, minced

1 (1-inch) piece fresh ginger, peeled and minced

1 carrot, peeled and thinly sliced

1 scallion, sliced

Any remaining sugar snap peas, sliced

Any remaining shiitake mushrooms, sliced

1 tablespoon soy sauce

½ teaspoon toasted sesame oil

2 cups cooked black rice

Any remaining baby spinach

1 Soy Sauce Jammy Egg (page 86), halved

Toasted sesame seeds

¼ cup microgreens

In a large skillet, heat the grapeseed oil over medium-high heat and add the garlic and ginger. Sauté for 2 minutes until soft and fragrant.

Add the carrot, scallion, sugar snap peas, and mushrooms, and sauté for 2 minutes until the carrot is tender. Add the soy sauce, sesame oil, and rice and cook, tossing, for another minute. Stir in the spinach and cook until just wilted.

Transfer the rice to a bowl, top with the egg, and garnish with sesame seeds and microgreens.

This Week's Menu

Monday	QUINOA TABBOULEH BOWL WITH LAMB
Tuesday	CHICKPEA AND TOMATO STEW WITH COUSCOUS
Wednesday	CHOPPED SALAD WITH LAMB AND TABBOULEH
Thursday	CHICKPEA AND TOMATO STEW WITH LAMB AND ROASTED BELL PEPPERS
Friday	QUINOA BOWL WITH CRISPY CHICKPEAS

It's not nice to pick favorites, but this week's recipes just might be mine. Spices such as cinnamon, allspice, and cumin meet lamb, chickpeas, and tomatoes to make a week full of incredibly flavorful lunches inspired by Mediterranean cuisine. The week starts with a bowl based around an addictive Quinoa Tabbouleh that you won't believe is as good for you as it is. The Chickpea and Tomato Stew comes together in one pot in less than 20 minutes, and it just keeps getting better as the flavors have a chance to deepen and get cozy with each other during the week. All week you'll be topping your bowls with a super simple but satisfying Garlic Yogurt Sauce; it brings a rich, bright zing to everything it touches. Set aside a few minutes on Wednesday night to make the Slow-Roasted Bell Peppers and Spiced Crispy Chickpeas. Neither requires a lot of hands-on time and they'll make Thursday's and Friday's lunches sing.

Grocery List

Make sure you have the following ingredients for the week.

Pantry

1 ½ cups quinoa

1 cup couscous

2 (14-ounce) cans chickpeas

1 (14-ounce) can diced tomatoes

1 ½ cups chicken stock (ideally homemade, see page 18) or water

Extra virgin olive oil

Grapeseed oil

2 tablespoons white wine vinegar

1 tablespoon tahini

1 tablespoon tomato paste

1 tablespoon capers

1 ½ teaspoons cinnamon

1 teaspoon allspice

1 teaspoon cumin seeds

½ teaspoon turmeric

2 tablespoons hemp seeds

¼ cup golden raisins

Produce

1 large bunch mint

1 bunch parsley

1 bunch scallions

2 lemons

7 garlic cloves

2 shallots

1 large carrot

2 bell peppers, any color

1 small zucchini

1 pint cherry tomatoes

½ cup pomegranate seeds

1 head romaine lettuce

Dairy

¾ cup full-fat Greek yogurt

Meat

1 pound ground lamb

Sunday Prep

Make the following recipes:

1 Garlic Yogurt Sauce (see opposite)

2 Quinoa Tabbouleh (see opposite)

3 Chickpea and Tomato Stew (page 102)

4 Spiced Lamb (page 104)

5 Spiced Crispy Chickpeas (page 105) WED

6 Slow-Roasted Bell Peppers (page 106) WED

Prepare and store in sealable containers in the refrigerator:

● Quinoa: In a medium saucepan, bring 3 cups of salted water to a boil. Add 1½ cups of quinoa, reduce to a simmer and cook, covered, for 15 minutes or until the water has evaporated. Turn off the heat, fluff with a fork, cover again, and let steam for 5 minutes. Makes 3¾ cups of cooked quinoa.

● Couscous: In a medium saucepan, bring 1 cup of salted water to a boil and add 1 tablespoon of olive oil. Add 1 cup of couscous, turn off the heat, and let sit for 5 minutes. Remove the lid and fluff with a fork. Makes 3 cups of cooked couscous.

● Drain and rinse all the chickpeas and dry them well. Store in an airtight container in the refrigerator. Makes 3½ cups.

Garlic Yogurt Sauce

✿ Makes about ¾ cup ✿

¾ cup full-fat Greek yogurt

1 tablespoon tahini

1 garlic clove, grated

Zest and juice of ½ lemon

¼ teaspoon kosher salt

In a bowl, mix all the ingredients together until well combined and smooth. Store in a covered jar in the refrigerator.

Quinoa Tabbouleh

✿ Makes 2½ cups ✿

---

2 cups parsley leaves and tender stems

1 cup mint leaves

4 scallions

3 tablespoons extra virgin olive oil

Zest and juice of 1 lemon

2 cups cooked quinoa

Kosher salt

Finely chop the parsley, mint, and scallions. Transfer them to a large bowl and add the oil and lemon zest and juice. Toss in the quinoa and stir to combine. Season with salt to taste. Store in an airtight container in the refrigerator.

Chickpea and Tomato Stew

✿ Makes 2 servings ✿

2 tablespoons extra virgin olive oil

1 shallot, chopped

3 garlic cloves, chopped

1 large carrot, peeled and diced

¼ cup golden raisins

1 tablespoon tomato paste

½ teaspoon kosher salt

½ teaspoon turmeric

½ teaspoon cinnamon

¼ teaspoon cumin seeds, ground

1 (14-ounce) can diced tomatoes

1½ cups chicken stock

2½ cups chickpeas

Zest of ½ lemon

In a medium Dutch oven or heavy-bottomed saucepan over medium heat, heat the oil. Add the shallot, garlic, and carrot. Sauté for 2 to 3 minutes until everything starts to soften. Add the raisins, tomato paste, salt, turmeric, cinnamon, and cumin seeds and stir to combine.

Add the tomatoes, stock, and chickpeas and simmer for 10 to 12 minutes, stirring often, until some of the liquid has evaporated and the stew has thickened. When stirring, mash a few of the chickpeas on the side of the pot, which will help thicken the stew.

Turn off the heat and stir in the lemon zest. Store in an airtight container in the refrigerator.

✿ **If the stew is too thick when you're reheating it, simply add some water or stock. Some chicken stock brands are saltier than others, whereas homemade ideally has no salt at all. This recipe starts with only ½ teaspoon of salt to account for that. Taste your stew at the end and if you feel as though it's missing something, it's most likely salt.**

Spiced Lamb

✿ Makes 3 servings ✿

1 tablespoon grapeseed oil

1 shallot, finely chopped

1 pound ground lamb

½ teaspoon kosher salt

½ teaspoon cinnamon

½ teaspoon allspice

½ teaspoon cumin seeds, ground

In a large skillet over medium heat, heat the oil and add the shallot. Cook for 2 minutes until soft and translucent. Add the lamb, breaking it up with a wooden spoon. Cook the lamb for 10 minutes, continuously stirring and breaking up any large chunks.

Add the salt, cinnamon, allspice, and cumin seeds and cook for another 1 to 2 minutes. The lamb should be darker in color and starting to crisp at the edges.

Turn off the heat and, using a slotted spoon, transfer the lamb to an airtight container, leaving any excess fat behind. Store in the refrigerator.

Spiced Crispy Chickpeas

☼ Makes 1 serving ☼

1 cup chickpeas, dried well

1 tablespoon grapeseed oil

⅛ teaspoon kosher salt

⅛ teaspoon cinnamon

⅛ teaspoon allspice

⅛ teaspoon cumin seeds, ground

Heat the oven to 350°F. In a medium bowl, toss all the ingredients together and stir to combine.

Place the chickpeas on a rimmed baking sheet in an even layer and transfer to the oven. Bake for 50 minutes to 1 hour, shaking the pan halfway through, until the chickpeas have crisped and are golden.

Transfer the chickpeas to a container and store at room temperature, with the lid slightly ajar to let any moisture escape.

Slow-Roasted Bell Peppers

✿ Makes 1 cup ✿

2 bell peppers—cored, seeded, and cut into thick slices

3 garlic cloves, halved

1 tablespoon capers

3 tablespoons extra virgin olive oil

1 teaspoon kosher salt

Heat the oven to 350°F. Place the peppers, garlic, and capers in a baking dish, drizzle with the oil and sprinkle with salt. Toss well to combine.

Roast for 45 minutes to 1 hour, stirring occasionally, until the peppers are very soft and slightly caramelized. Store in an airtight container in the refrigerator.

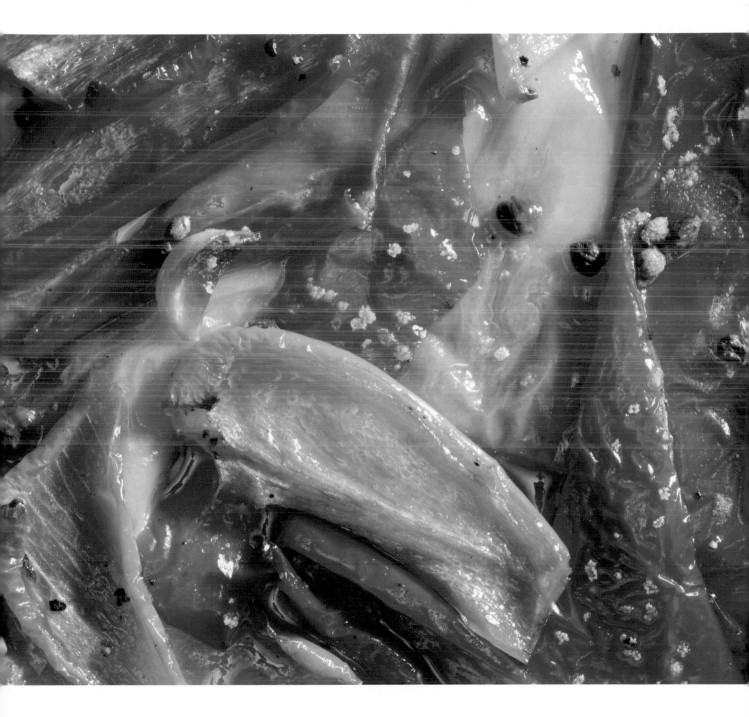

Quinoa Tabbouleh Bowl with Lamb

2 cups Quinoa Tabbouleh (page 101)

1 serving Spiced Lamb (page 104)

½ small zucchini, thinly sliced

4 to 5 cherry tomatoes, quartered

2 tablespoons Garlic Yogurt Sauce (page 101)

2 tablespoons pomegranate seeds

Torn mint leaves

Torn parsley leaves

Make a bed of tabbouleh in the bottom of a bowl.

Top with the lamb, zucchini, and tomatoes.

Spoon the yogurt sauce in the middle and sprinkle with the pomegranate seeds, mint, and parsley.

Chickpea and Tomato Stew
with Couscous

1 ½ cups cooked couscous

1 serving Chickpea and Tomato Stew (page 102)

3 tablespoons Garlic Yogurt Sauce (page 101)

2 tablespoons pomegranate seeds

Torn mint leaves

Torn parsley leaves

Make a bed of couscous in the bottom of a bowl.

Top with the chickpea and tomato stew, followed by the yogurt sauce.

Garnish with the pomegranate seeds, mint, and parsley.

Chopped Salad with Lamb and Tabbouleh

1 tablespoon Garlic Yogurt Sauce (page 101)

1 tablespoon extra virgin olive oil

1 tablespoon white wine vinegar

½ head romaine lettuce, trimmed and chopped

½ small zucchini, diced

5 cherry tomatoes, quartered

1 scallion, finely chopped

Hemp seeds

2 tablespoons pomegranate seeds

½ cup Quinoa Tabbouleh (page 101)

1 serving Spiced Lamb (page 104)

Torn mint leaves

Torn parsley leaves

Black pepper

In a small bowl, whisk together the yogurt sauce, oil, and vinegar. Set aside.

Place the lettuce, zucchini, tomatoes, scallion, hemp seeds, and pomegranate seeds in the bottom of a bowl and drizzle with the yogurt dressing.

Top with the quinoa tabbouleh and lamb.

Garnish with more hemp seeds, mint, parsley, and a few grinds of black pepper.

Chickpea and Tomato Stew with Lamb and Roasted Bell Peppers

1 serving Chickpea and Tomato Stew (page 102)

1 serving Spiced Lamb (page 104)

1½ cups cooked couscous

½ cup Slow-Roasted Bell Peppers (page 106)

3 tablespoons Garlic Yogurt Sauce (page 101)

Torn mint leaves

Torn parsley leaves

In a small saucepan over medium heat, heat the chickpea stew and lamb together until just warmed through.

Make a bed of couscous in the bottom of a bowl. Top with the stew, followed by the roasted peppers.

Top with the yogurt sauce and garnish with mint and parsley.

Quinoa Bowl with Crispy Chickpeas

1½ cups cooked quinoa

½ head romaine lettuce, trimmed and chopped

5 cherry tomatoes, quartered

1 scallion, chopped

1 tablespoon extra virgin olive oil

1 tablespoon white wine vinegar

1 serving Spiced Crispy Chickpeas (page 105)

½ cup Slow-Roasted Bell Peppers (page 106)

2 tablespoons pomegranate seeds

2 tablespoons Garlic Yogurt Sauce (page 101)

Hemp seeds

Torn mint leaves

Torn parsley leaves

Place the quinoa, lettuce, tomatoes, and scallion in the bottom of a bowl. Drizzle with the oil and vinegar.

Top with the chickpeas, roasted peppers, pomegranate seeds, and yogurt sauce.

Garnish with hemp seeds, mint, and parsley.

This Week's Menu

Monday	FISH TACO BOWL
Tuesday	CHICKEN CHILI VERDE WITH AVOCADO
Wednesday	CHICKEN CHILI VERDE WITH BLACK BEANS AND SPICY SLAW
Thursday	KALE SALAD WITH CHICKEN AND ROASTED CARROTS
Friday	CRUNCHY TUNA SALAD WITH ROASTED CARROTS

This week starts off with a few more Sunday prep tasks than usual—but that's a good thing! Making these simple recipes will lead to a week when the lunches almost make themselves. You'll have all your ingredients and elements prepped and waiting for you in the refrigerator, ready to be layered into your bowls. The Chicken Chili Verde is bound to become a repeat in your recipe rotation. All the cooking happens in one pot, and the result is a savory stew that's just asking to be topped with avocado, yogurt, and pepitas. The base for a crunchy green slaw this week is a creamy, bright, and spicy jalapeño dressing, which I promise is so good you'll want to make more salads just so you can use it again. If your knife skills are lacking and you can't cut the jalapeño into small enough pieces, feel free to give the dressing a whirl in a blender or food processor.

Grocery List

Make sure you have the following ingredients for the week.

Pantry

Avocado oil

2 tablespoons mayonnaise

1 (14-ounce) can black beans, rinsed and
    drained

2 ½ cups brown rice

¾ cup pepitas

1 teaspoon cumin seeds

1 (5-ounce) can olive oil–packed tuna

Produce

5 garlic cloves

3 limes

5 jalapeños

1 pound tomatillos

1 small white onion

1 poblano pepper

1 bunch cilantro

1 small head green cabbage

1 bunch scallions

4 large carrots

1 ripe avocado

4 radishes

1 (5-ounce) container baby kale

Dairy

½ cup full-fat Greek yogurt

2 tablespoons butter

Meat and Seafood

5 bone-in, skin-on chicken thighs (about
    1 ½ pounds)

1 (¼ pound) fillet firm white fish (halibut, cod,
    or sea bass)

If you are only able to buy radishes by the bunch,
go for it. You can slice them up and garnish any and
all bowls with it.

Sunday Prep

Make the following recipes:

1 Chicken Chili Verde (page 122)

2 Creamy Jalapeño Dressing (page 124)

3 Spicy Green Slaw (page 124)

4 Doctored-Up Black Beans (page 126)

5 Cumin-Roasted Carrots (page 127) WED

Prepare and store in sealable containers in the refrigerator:

- Brown rice: Bring a medium saucepan of salted water to a boil. Add 2½ cups of brown rice, reduce to a simmer, and cook for 25 to 30 minutes until the rice is tender and slightly chewy. Drain in a fine-mesh strainer. Makes about 4 cups of cooked rice.

- Marinated fish: Place the fish fillet on a sheet of aluminum foil. Top with 1 tablespoon of butter, the zest of ½ lime, a pinch of salt, and a few grinds of black pepper. Wrap the foil over the fish and let it marinate in the refrigerator until ready to roast.

- Shredded cabbage: Discard any discolored or wilted outer leaves. Quarter and core the cabbage head. Using a mandoline or a sharp knife, shred the cabbage into thin slaw-like pieces. Makes about 5 cups of shredded cabbage.

- Toasted pepitas: Place all the pepitas in a skillet. Heat over medium-high heat, shaking often, until they become slightly golden, about 1 minute.

Chicken Chili Verde

✿ Makes 2 servings ✿

5 bone-in, skin-on chicken thighs (about 1½ pounds), skin removed and reserved

1 pound tomatillos, husked and rinsed

2 jalapeños

1 poblano pepper

3 garlic cloves, peeled

1 small white onion, peeled and halved

1 small bunch cilantro (about 20 sprigs)

2 teaspoons kosher salt

2 tablespoons avocado oil or rendered chicken fat (use the fat if you can)

To render chicken fat (optional, but recommended): In a nonstick skillet, place the reserved chicken skin in an even layer and turn the heat to medium low. Cook the skin for about 25 to 30 minutes, tossing often, until it is completely crispy and golden. Remove the crispy skin from the pan, and pour the rendered fat into a jar and set aside. Transfer the skin to a plate and reserve for garnish.

Turn the oven broiler on high. Place the tomatillos, jalapeños, poblano, garlic, and onion on a rimmed baking sheet and place it in the oven on the top rack. Broil for 3 to 6 minutes until the vegetables are charred. Remove the vegetables from the oven, discard the jalapeño and poblano stems, and transfer everything to a blender. Add the cilantro and salt. Blend until smooth, then set aside.

it you can)

½ teaspoon cumin seeds, lightly ground

In a Dutch oven or a heavy-bottomed pan over medium heat, heat 2 tablespoons of oil or the reserved rendered chicken fat. Place the chicken in the pan and fry for 2 to 3 minutes on each side until golden brown. Transfer to a plate. Turn the heat down to medium low and add the cumin seeds, then pour in the tomatillo sauce. Bring the sauce to a simmer and return the chicken thighs to the pan. Cook for 35 to 40 minutes, covered, until the meat comes away from the bone easily.

Transfer the chicken to a plate and shred the meat, discarding the bones. Reserve about ½ cup for use later in the week and store it in the refrigerator. Add the rest of the meat back to the pan and cook, uncovered, for another 8 to 10 minutes until the sauce is slightly thickened. Once cool, pour it into an airtight container and store in the refrigerator.

tip

Don't forget to reserve ½ cup of shredded chicken from this recipe for use later in the week. If you render the chicken skin, as described here, you can use it either in this recipe or in the future. It adds incredible flavor to almost any dish. This amount of skin will render out about 3 tablespoons of fat.

Creamy Jalapeño Dressing

✿ Makes ½ cup ✿

---

1 garlic clove, grated

Zest and juice of 1 lime

1 jalapeño, minced (seeds removed for milder heat)

¼ cup avocado oil

2 tablespoons full-fat Greek yogurt

1 tablespoon mayonnaise

½ teaspoon kosher salt

Mix all the ingredients together in a jar and store in the refrigerator.

Spicy Green Slaw

✿ Makes 3 cups ✿

---

4 cups shredded cabbage

3 scallions, minced

1 handful cilantro, chopped

2 tablespoons Creamy Jalapeño Dressing

Kosher salt

In a large bowl, combine all the ingredients, then season with salt to taste. Store in an airtight container in the refrigerator.

Doctored-Up Black Beans

✿ Makes 1½ cups ✿

1 tablespoon butter or rendered chicken fat

1 garlic clove, minced

½ jalapeño, minced

1 (14-ounce) can black beans, rinsed and drained

¼ teaspoon kosher salt

2 teaspoons lime juice (from about ¼ lime)

In a small saucepan over medium heat, heat the butter, garlic, and jalapeño. Sauté until the vegetables have softened and are translucent.

Add the beans, salt, and ¼ cup of water. Cook for 3 minutes over low heat until some of the water has evaporated. Turn off the heat and stir in the lime juice. Store in an airtight container in the refrigerator.

Cumin-Roasted Carrots

✿ Makes 2 cups ✿

4 large carrots, peeled and sliced on the diagonal into ¼-inch slices

2 tablespoons avocado oil

½ teaspoon cumin seeds, lightly ground

½ teaspoon kosher salt

Heat the oven to 425°F. Place the carrots on a rimmed baking sheet and drizzle with the oil. Sprinkle with the cumin seeds and salt.

Roast the carrots for 20 to 25 minutes until they are tender and browned. Store in an airtight container in the refrigerator.

Spread the carrots out as far apart from each other as possible—it will make them roast rather than steam, giving you that delicious caramelized finish. If necessary, divide them between two baking sheets for best results.

Fish Taco Bowl

1 marinated white fish fillet

1½ cups cooked brown rice

¾ cup Doctored-Up Black Beans (page 126)

1 cup Spicy Green Slaw (page 124)

½ avocado, sliced

Torn cilantro leaves

1 radish, thinly sliced

1 lime wedge

Turn the oven broiler to high and place a rack in the highest position. Line a baking sheet or small baking dish with aluminum foil.

Unwrap the fish and place it on the baking sheet. Broil for 2 to 3 minutes until it starts to brown. Turn off the broiler and heat the oven to 450°F. Bake the fish for another 4 to 5 minutes until it flakes easily when tested with a fork. Remove the fish from the oven and set aside.

Place the rice and beans in the bottom of a bowl. Add the slaw and avocado. Place the fish on top and garnish with cilantro, radish, and a lime wedge.

Chicken Chili Verde with Avocado

1 ½ cups cooked brown rice

1 serving Chicken Chili Verde (page 122)

½ avocado, sliced

2 tablespoons full-fat Greek yogurt

1 radish, thinly sliced

Torn cilantro leaves

Toasted pepitas

Crispy chicken skin (optional, but strongly encouraged)

Place the rice in the bottom of a bowl and add the chicken chili verde.

Top with the avocado and yogurt.

Garnish with the radish, cilantro, pepitas, and chicken skin (if using).

Chicken Chili Verde with Black Beans and Spicy Slaw

1 cup cooked brown rice

¾ cup Doctored-Up Black Beans (page 126)

1 serving Chicken Chili Verde (page 122)

1 cup Spicy Green Slaw (page 124)

2 tablespoons full-fat Greek yogurt

Toasted pepitas

Place the rice and beans in the bottom of a bowl and add the chicken chili verde.

Top with the slaw and yogurt.

Garnish with pepitas.

Kale Salad with Chicken and Roasted Carrots

2 cups baby kale

2 tablespoons Creamy Jalapeño Dressing (page 124)

½ cup shredded chicken (reserved from Chicken Chili Verde recipe, page 122)

1 cup Cumin-Roasted Carrots (page 127)

½ cup Spicy Green Slaw (page 124)

1 scallion, sliced

1 radish, thinly sliced

Torn cilantro leaves

Toasted pepitas

Place the kale in the bottom of a bowl and drizzle with the dressing.

Top with the chicken, carrots, slaw, and scallion.

Garnish with the radish, cilantro, and pepitas.

Crunchy Tuna Salad with Roasted Carrots

1 tablespoon mayonnaise

Juice of ½ lime

Kosher salt

Black pepper

1 cup shredded cabbage, finely chopped

1 tablespoon chopped cilantro, plus torn leaves

1 small jalapeño, seeded and minced

1 radish, cut into matchsticks

1 scallion, finely chopped

1 (5-ounce) can wild-caught tuna in olive oil, drained

2 cups baby kale

2 tablespoons Creamy Jalapeño Dressing (page 124)

1 cup Cumin-Roasted Carrots (page 127)

Toasted pepitas

In a medium bowl, whisk together the mayo, lime juice, a pinch of salt, and a few grinds of pepper.

Add the cabbage, cilantro, jalapeño, radish, and scallion. Flake in the tuna and mix well. Set aside.

Place the kale in the bottom of a bowl and drizzle with the dressing. Top with the tuna salad and roasted carrots. Garnish with cilantro leaves and pepitas.

This Week's Menu

Monday   RICE BOWL WITH PORK RADICCHIO CUPS

Tuesday   NORI ROLLS WITH AVOCADO AND SPROUTS

Wednesday   NORI ROLLS WITH PORK AND SPICY MAYO

Thursday   NORI ROLLS WITH MUSHROOMS AND KIMCHI

Friday   KIMCHI UDON WITH AN EGG

Bursting with Asian flavors and textures, this week's menu is here to shake up the lunch routine. On Monday, start the week with intensely savory pork lettuce cups made creamy by sliced avocado. For the next few days, you'll be making nori rolls—Japanese-style hand rolls wrapped in nori seaweed sheets. Tuesday's lunch is a fresh and crisp veggie-filled version, followed by a spicy pork-filled version on Wednesday. On Thursday, it's an umami mushroom-and-sprout-filled roll, while Friday's kimchi noodles are an excellent way to celebrate the end of the work week. The best part? They keep beautifully if they're made the night before. If you're not so familiar with kimchi, that's okay! This recipe is a really good primer on the funky fermented Korean condiment. Not only does the stuff taste amazing, but it's also packed with gut-healthy probiotics. Go ahead and eat the rest right out of the jar!

Grocery List

Make sure you have the following ingredients for the week.

Pantry

1½ cups white rice (jasmine or short grain)

3 ounces udon noodles or spaghetti (dry or frozen)

Avocado oil

2 tablespoons fish sauce

½ cup soy sauce, plus 6 takeout soy sauce packets

1 tablespoon tahini

2 tablespoons toasted sesame oil

¼ cup plus 1 teaspoon rice wine vinegar

1 ounce (about 1 cup) dehydrated shiitake mushrooms

½ cup roasted salted peanuts

¼ cup sesame seeds

7 sheets nori seaweed

¼ cup mayonnaise

2 teaspoons Sriracha

¼ cup hemp seeds

1 (16-ounce) jar kimchi

Produce

2 garlic cloves

1 small onion

1 (2-inch) piece fresh ginger

1 red bell pepper

1 lime

1 bunch chives

1 bunch cilantro

1 pound broccoli

2 avocados

3 carrots (or 1½ cups preshredded carrots)

1 head radicchio

1½ cups sprouts or microgreens

1 (5-ounce) container baby salad greens (arugula, kale, or similar)

1 Persian cucumber

Dairy

1 tablespoon butter

1 egg

Meat

1 pound ground pork

Sunday Prep

Make the following recipes:

1 Sesame Dressing (see opposite)

2 Roasted Broccoli with Peanuts (see opposite)

3 Pork with Chives (page 143)

4 Soy-Marinated Shiitake Mushrooms (page 144)

Prepare and store in sealable containers in the refrigerator:

● Rice: In a medium saucepan, bring 3 cups of salted water to a boil. Add 1½ cups of rice, cover, reduce to a simmer, and cook for 17 minutes without lifting the lid. Turn off the heat and let the rice sit with the lid on for 5 minutes. Fluff with a fork and stir in 1 teaspoon of rice wine vinegar and ¼ teaspoon of toasted sesame oil. Makes about 3 cups of cooked rice.

● Spicy mayo: Combine ¼ cup of mayo with 2 teaspoons of Sriracha (more if you like it very spicy).

● If using whole carrots: Shred all the carrots using a mandoline, or cut them into thin matchsticks with a sharp knife. Makes about 1½ cups of shredded carrots.

● Toasted sesame seeds: Place all the sesame seeds in a clean, dry skillet. Turn the heat up to medium and toast, shaking often, until the seeds become light golden brown, about 2 to 3 minutes.

Sesame Dressing

☼ Makes ¼ cup ☼

1 tablespoon tahini

3 teaspoons toasted sesame oil

1 teaspoon soy sauce

2 tablespoons rice wine vinegar

1 tablespoon avocado oil

¼ teaspoon kosher salt

Combine all the ingredients in a jar, close the lid, and shake well. Store in the refrigerator.

Roasted Broccoli with Peanuts

☼ Makes 2 cups ☼

1 pound broccoli, cut into florets

1 garlic clove, finely chopped

2 tablespoons avocado oil

1 tablespoon fish sauce

Kosher salt

Zest of ½ lime

¼ cup roasted salted peanuts, chopped

Heat the oven to 425°F. Combine the broccoli, garlic, oil, and fish sauce on a rimmed baking sheet. Season with salt and toss until combined.

Transfer to the oven and roast for 15 to 20 minutes, or until the broccoli is tender and browned in spots. Remove the broccoli from the oven and sprinkle with the lime zest and peanuts. Store in an airtight container in the refrigerator.

Pork with Chives

✿ Makes 2 servings ✿

1 tablespoon avocado oil

1 garlic clove, minced

½ small onion, finely chopped

1 (1-inch) piece fresh ginger, peeled and minced

1 pound ground pork

½ red bell pepper, finely chopped

1 tablespoon fish sauce

2 teaspoons soy sauce

Kosher salt

1 tablespoon chopped chives

1 small bunch cilantro, chopped

Zest of ½ lime

In a large skillet over medium-high heat, heat the oil. Sauté the garlic, onion, and ginger for 2 minutes until soft. Add the pork and cook, breaking it up with a wooden spoon, for 6 minutes. Add the bell pepper, fish sauce, soy sauce, and a pinch of salt and cook for another 2 minutes. Turn off the heat and stir in the chives, cilantro, and lime zest.

Store in an airtight container in the refrigerator.

Soy-Marinated Shiitake Mushrooms

✿ Makes 1 cup ✿

1 ounce (about 1 cup) dehydrated shiitake mushrooms

¼ cup water

¼ cup soy sauce

2 tablespoons rice wine vinegar

1 (1-inch) piece fresh ginger, sliced into coins

1 teaspoon sugar

In a small saucepan, combine all the ingredients. Bring the mixture to a boil, reduce to a simmer, and cook for 5 minutes. Turn off the heat and let cool for 20 minutes.

Remove the mushrooms and discard the liquid. Slice the mushrooms and store them in a glass container in the refrigerator.

Rice Bowl with Pork Radicchio Cups

1 cup cooked rice

1 cup Roasted Broccoli with Peanuts (page 141)

¼ cup shredded carrots

½ avocado, sliced

¼ cup kimchi

1 tablespoon Sesame Dressing (page 141)

2 to 3 large radicchio leaves

1 serving Pork with Chives (page 143)

Chopped chives

Torn cilantro leaves

Toasted sesame seeds

1 lime wedge

Place the rice in the bottom of a bowl and top with the roasted broccoli, shredded carrots, avocado, and kimchi. Drizzle with the dressing.

Fill each radicchio leaf with equal amounts of the pork and place in the bowl.

Garnish with chives, cilantro, sesame seeds, and a lime wedge.

✿

TIP **Squeeze a bit of lime juice over the avocado to keep it from turning brown. You can also pack the avocado separately and add it right before eating.**

✿

Nori Rolls with Avocado and Sprouts

2 sheets nori seaweed

⅔ cup cooked rice

½ cup sprouts

½ avocado, sliced

1 Persian cucumber, quartered lengthwise

A few whole chives

2 teaspoons toasted sesame seeds

1 cup baby greens

1 cup Roasted Broccoli with Peanuts (page 141)

¼ cup shredded carrots

1 tablespoon Sesame Dressing (page 141)

Hemp seeds

2 takeout soy sauce packets

To make the nori rolls, place a sheet of nori on a clean work surface. Using your hands, spread half of the rice in an even layer on top of the nori, leaving a ½ inch border with no rice. Layer half of the sprouts, avocado, cucumber, chives, and sesame seeds in the bottom third of the nori sheet.

Gently but firmly roll the edge closest to you toward the center of the nori wrap, like a sushi roll. If things fall out of the sides, don't worry; you can push them back in later. When you get to the end of the roll, take a grain of rice and smush it on the very end of the nori, to act as glue. Repeat this in one or two more spots. Flip the roll over so the seam side is on the bottom, and gently pat down to seal everything. Using a sharp knife, cut the roll in half. Repeat with the other half of the ingredients.

Build a salad in the bowl: Place the greens in the bottom, and top with the broccoli and carrots. Drizzle the salad with the sesame dressing and garnish with hemp seeds. Place the nori rolls on top of the salad.

Pack the soy sauce packets with your lunch.

Nori Rolls with Pork and Spicy Mayo

2 sheets nori seaweed

⅔ cup cooked rice

1 serving Pork with Chives (page 143)

¼ cup shredded carrots

¼ cup sprouts

A few sprigs cilantro

2 tablespoons spicy mayo

1 cup baby greens

½ cup shredded radicchio

½ avocado, sliced

1 tablespoon minced chives

1 tablespoon Sesame Dressing (page 141)

Hemp seeds

2 takeout soy sauce packets

To make the nori rolls, place a sheet of nori on a clean work surface. Using your hands, spread half of the rice in an even layer on top of the nori, leaving a ½ inch border with no rice. Layer half of the pork, carrots, sprouts, and cilantro in the bottom third of the nori sheet. Drizzle with half of the spicy mayo.

Gently but firmly roll the edge closest to you toward the center of the nori wrap, like a sushi roll. If things fall out of the sides, don't worry; you can push them back in later. When you get to the end of the roll, take a grain of rice and smush it on the very end of the nori, to act as glue. Repeat this in one or two more spots. Flip the roll over so the seam side is on the bottom, and gently pat down to seal everything. Using a sharp knife, cut the roll in half. Repeat with the other half of the ingredients.

Build a salad in the bowl: Place the greens in the bottom, and top with the radicchio, avocado, and chives. Drizzle the salad with the sesame dressing and garnish with hemp seeds. Place the nori rolls on top of the salad.

Pack the soy sauce packets with your lunch.

Nori Rolls with Mushrooms and Kimchi

2 sheets nori seaweed

⅔ cup cooked rice

⅔ cup Soy-Marinated Shiitake Mushrooms (page 144)

¼ cup kimchi, drained and roughly chopped

½ cup sprouts

½ red bell pepper, thinly sliced

Any remaining radicchio, shredded

A few whole chives

2 tablespoons spicy mayo

1 cup baby greens

¼ cup shredded carrots

1 tablespoon Sesame Dressing (page 141)

Roasted salted peanuts, chopped

2 takeout soy sauce packets

To make the nori rolls, place a sheet of nori on a clean work surface. Using your hands, spread half of the rice in an even layer on top of the nori, leaving a ½ inch border with no rice. Layer half of the mushrooms, kimchi, sprouts, bell peppers, radicchio, and chives in the bottom third of the nori sheet. Drizzle with half of the spicy mayo.

Gently but firmly, roll the edge closest to you toward the center of the nori wrap, like a sushi roll. If things fall out of the sides, don't worry; you can push them back in later. When you get to the end, take a grain of rice and smush it on the very end of the nori, to act as glue. Repeat this in one or two more spots. Flip the roll over so the seam side is in the bottom, and gently pat down to seal everything. Using a sharp knife, cut the roll in half. Repeat with the other half of the ingredients.

Build a salad in the bowl: Place the greens in the bottom, and top with the carrots. Drizzle the salad with the sesame dressing and garnish with peanuts. Place the nori rolls on top of the salad.

Pack the soy sauce packets with your lunch.

Kimchi Udon with an Egg

Kosher salt

3 ounces udon noodles or spaghetti

1 tablespoon butter

1 egg

½ small onion, thinly sliced

¼ cup shredded carrots

⅓ cup Soy-Marinated Shiitake Mushrooms (page 144)

½ cup kimchi, roughly chopped, plus 2 tablespoons kimchi brine

½ teaspoon toasted sesame oil

1 teaspoon soy sauce

1 tablespoon chopped chives

1 sheet nori seaweed, cut into thin strips

Toasted sesame seeds

Any remaining sprouts (optional)

Bring a medium saucepan of salted water to a boil. Add the noodles and cook according to the package directions until al dente. Drain and set aside.

Meanwhile, in a medium skillet over medium high heat, heat the butter. Once it's melted, crack the egg into the pan and make a sunny-side up egg. Cook for 2 to 3 minutes until the white is set and the yolk is still runny. Using a spatula, transfer the egg to a plate and set aside, leaving the pan slightly greasy.

Add the onion and carrot to the pan and sauté for 3 minutes until both are soft. Add the mushrooms, kimchi and its brine, oil, and soy sauce. Remove from the heat, add the noodles and chives, and toss to combine. Place the noodles in a bowl and top with the egg.

Garnish with the nori, sesame seeds, and sprouts (if using).

Week 8   Lentils + Shrimp + Celery

This Week's Menu

Monday	LENTIL BOWL WITH ROASTED SHRIMP AND CELERY ROOT
Tuesday	CHOPPED SALAD WITH SHRIMP, ASPARAGUS, AND GOAT CHEESE
Wednesday	SHRIMP SALAD WITH HERB CRACKERS
Thursday	CHICKEN SCHNITZEL WITH LENTIL SALAD
Friday	CHOPPED SALAD WITH CHICKEN AND ASPARAGUS MIMOSA

This chapter gets its refined flavors from some classic French components: Lentil Salad, Caramelized Celery Root, and Shallot Vinaigrette. The lentil salad is full of fiber and good-for-you vegetables and will have you daydreaming about picnicking along the Seine. Topping it with celery root and shrimp creates lunches that are light but bursting with flavor. When shopping for celery root a.k.a celeriac, look for one that is firm, not squishy, and feels heavy for its size (although the vegetable looks ugly, it has a beautiful, mild flavor). Wednesday's shrimp salad, an often-overlooked dish of the past, gets a face-lift with the addition of this week's herb of choice: dill. Later in the week, lunches bulk up with the addition of chicken schnitzel. Rolled in a combo of panko, dill, fennel seeds, and caraway seeds, these crispy cutlets are great hot right out of the pan but also delightful at room temperature or cold. All the dishes this week really benefit from a hit of fresh lemon juice right before eating; feel free to tuck a lemon wedge in your bowl before sealing the lid.

Grocery List

Make sure you have the following ingredients for the week.

Pantry

Extra virgin olive oil

Grapeseed oil

3 tablespoons white or red wine vinegar

1 tablespoon mayonnaise

1 tablespoon whole-grain mustard

2 teaspoons fennel seeds

1 teaspoon caraway seeds

1½ cups green lentils

1 cup panko breadcrumbs

½ cup walnuts

5 to 7 herb crackers (store-bought or homemade, page 220)

Produce

1 bunch celery

1 carrot

2 shallots

2 garlic cloves

1 bunch dill

1 lemon

1 medium celery root

1 bunch asparagus

2 heads butter lettuce or 1 large head romaine lettuce

3 golden beets (or red beets)

Dairy

2 eggs

4 ounces goat cheese

Meat and Seafood

¾ pound (about 18 pieces) shrimp—peeled, deveined, and frozen until ready to use

2 boneless, skinless chicken breasts (about 1 pound)

Sunday Prep

Make the following recipes:

1 Shallot Vinaigrette (see opposite)

2 Roasted Lemon Shrimp (page 160)

3 Lentil Salad (page 162)

4 Caramelized Celery Root (page 163)

5 Chicken Schnitzel with Fennel and Caraway (page 164) WED

Prepare and store in sealable containers in the refrigerator:

Roast the beets by using the technique on page 45.

Hard-boiled egg: Bring a small saucepan of water to a boil. Using a spoon, carefully add 1 egg. Boil for 10 minutes. Rinse with cold water before storing.

Chopped toasted walnuts: Place all the walnuts in a clean, dry skillet. Turn the heat on medium and toast, shaking often, until the walnuts become a shade darker. Let them cool, then chop them up.

Shallot Vinaigrette

½ shallot, minced

¼ cup extra virgin olive oil

3 tablespoons white or red wine vinegar

1 tablespoon whole-grain mustard

¾ teaspoon kosher salt

Combine all the ingredients in a glass jar, seal with a lid, and give it a good shake. Store in the refrigerator.

✿

TIP **If your knife skills aren't awesome and your shallot pieces are too chunky, blitz the vinaigrette with an immersion blender or in a food processor.**

✿

Roasted Lemon Shrimp

✿ Makes about 18 shrimp
(about 3 servings of 5 to 6 shrimp) ✿

¾ pound shrimp (about 18 pieces), defrosted if frozen

1 tablespoon grapeseed oil

Kosher salt

Black pepper

Zest and juice of ½ lemon

Heat the oven to 450°F. Place the shrimp on a rimmed baking sheet. Pour the oil over the shrimp and season with salt, a few grinds of black pepper, and the lemon zest.

Toss to combine and spread the shrimp out in a single layer. Transfer to the oven and roast for 3 minutes on each side. Remove the pan from the oven and drizzle with the lemon juice.

Let the shrimp cool before storing in an airtight container in the refrigerator.

Lentil Salad

☼ Makes 3 cups ☼

1 tablespoon grapeseed oil

2 garlic cloves, chopped

1 shallot, finely chopped

2 celery ribs, finely diced

1 carrot, peeled and finely diced

1 ½ cups green lentils

½ teaspoon kosher salt

3 tablespoons Shallot Vinaigrette (page 159)

¼ cup dill, chopped

In a medium saucepan over medium heat, heat the oil, garlic, shallot, celery, and carrot. Cook for 5 minutes, stirring often, until the vegetables are soft. Add the lentils, salt, and enough water to cover the ingredients by 2 inches. Bring the mixture to a boil, reduce to a simmer, and cook for 25 to 35 minutes.

At 25 minutes, taste a few lentils for doneness; they should be tender but not falling apart. Turn off the heat, drain the lentil mixture in a fine-mesh strainer, and return it to the pan. Pour in the vinaigrette, add the dill, and stir everything together until well combined. Store in an airtight container in the refrigerator.

Caramelized Celery Root

✿ Makes 2 cups ✿

1 medium celery root, peeled and cut into 1-inch cubes

1 tablespoon grapeseed oil

Kosher salt

Black pepper

Heat the oven to 425°F. Place the celery root cubes on a rimmed baking sheet. Drizzle the oil on top and season with salt and a few grinds of pepper. Toss to combine well and transfer to the oven.

Roast for 15 to 20 minutes, tossing once or twice, until the cubes are fork-tender and golden. Store in an airtight container in the refrigerator.

Celery root, the actual root of a celery plant, can be intimidating because of its gnarly appearance. But underneath all that rough brown skin is a wonderful root vegetable similar in texture to a parsnip and with a faint celery taste. It can also be boiled and pureed like potatoes.

Chicken Schnitzel with Fennel and Caraway

✿ Makes 4 pieces ✿

1 large egg, beaten

1 cup panko breadcrumbs

¼ cup dill, finely chopped

1 teaspoon kosher salt

2 teaspoons fennel seeds, lightly ground

1 teaspoon caraway seeds, lightly ground

2 boneless, skinless chicken breasts (about 1 pound), cut in half lengthwise

¼ cup grapeseed oil

In a shallow bowl, beat the egg with 1 tablespoon of water. In a separate shallow bowl, combine the breadcrumbs, dill, salt, fennel seeds, and caraway seeds. Dip a piece of chicken in the egg and let the excess drip off. Place the chicken in the breadcrumb mixture and press it in until both sides are evenly coated. Transfer to a rimmed baking sheet and repeat with the remaining chicken.

In a large skillet over medium-high heat, heat the oil until hot but not smoking. Test the oil by dropping in a few breadcrumbs; when they sizzle, the oil is ready.

Working in batches, place each piece of chicken in the oil and fry until golden, 2 to 3 minutes, adjusting the heat as you go. Carefully flip each cutlet and repeat on the other side. Transfer each cutlet to a plate.

Store the chicken by wrapping 2 pieces together in aluminum foil. Reheat in a 350°F oven for 10 minutes when you're ready to eat or before assembling your lunch.

Lentil Bowl with Roasted Shrimp and Celery Root

1½ cups **Lentil Salad (page 162)**

1 cup **Caramelized Celery Root (page 163)**

1 **Roasted Golden Beet, quartered**

1 teaspoon **Shallot Vinaigrette (page 159)**

5 to 6 **Roasted Lemon Shrimp (page 160)**

Torn dill fronds

1 lemon wedge

Place the lentil salad in the bottom of a bowl.

Add the celery root and beets, then drizzle the vinaigrette over the vegetables.

Top with the shrimp and garnish with dill and lemon wedge.

Chopped Salad with Shrimp, Asparagus, and Goat Cheese

Kosher salt

½ bunch asparagus, trimmed and cut into 3-inch pieces

3 cups chopped butter lettuce or romaine

2 tablespoons Shallot Vinaigrette (page 159)

5 or 6 Roasted Lemon Shrimp (page 160)

1 cup Caramelized Celery Root (page 163)

1 Roasted Golden Beet, quartered

2 celery ribs, thinly sliced

2 tablespoons chopped toasted walnuts

2 ounces goat cheese, crumbled

Black pepper

Bring a small saucepan of salted water to a boil. Add the asparagus and blanch for 30 seconds to 1 minute, depending on the thickness; it should be tender but still crisp. Immediately drain the asparagus and rinse it with cold water. Set aside.

Place the lettuce in the bottom of a bowl and drizzle with the vinaigrette.

Top with the asparagus, shrimp, celery root, beet, celery, walnuts, and goat cheese.

Season the salad with a few grinds of pepper.

Shrimp Salad with Herb Crackers

1 rib celery, finely chopped, plus tender leaves

½ shallot, minced

A few sprigs of dill fronds, chopped

1 tablespoon mayonnaise

1 teaspoon lemon juice

Black pepper

5 to 6 Roasted Lemon Shrimp (page 160), tails removed and cut in half

1 cup butter lettuce or romaine lettuce leaves

1 teaspoon Shallot Vinaigrette (page 159)

5 to 7 herb crackers, for serving

In a small bowl, combine the celery, shallot, dill, mayo, lemon juice, and a few grinds of pepper. Add the shrimp and toss to combine.

Place the lettuce in the bottom of a bowl and drizzle with the vinaigrette. Top with the shrimp salad.

Pack the crackers separately and enjoy with your lunch.

Chicken Schnitzel with Lentil Salad

1½ cups Lentil Salad (page 162)

1 celery rib, very thinly sliced, plus any remaining tender leaves

1 Roasted Golden Beet, quartered

1 teaspoon Shallot Vinaigrette (page 159)

2 pieces Chicken Schnitzel (page 164), cut into thick slices

Chopped toasted walnuts

Torn dill fronds

1 lemon wedge

Place the lentil salad in the bottom of a bowl and top with the celery, celery leaves, and beet. Drizzle with the vinaigrette.

Top with the chicken and garnish with the walnuts, dill, and lemon wedge.

Chopped Salad with Chicken and Asparagus Mimosa

Kosher salt

½ bunch asparagus, trimmed

3 cups chopped butter lettuce or romaine lettuce

2 tablespoons Shallot Vinaigrette (page 159)

1 hard-boiled egg

Black pepper

2 pieces Chicken Schnitzel (page 164), cut into thick slices

2 ounces goat cheese, crumbled

Chopped toasted walnuts

Torn dill fronds

1 lemon wedge

Bring a small saucepan of salted water to a boil. Add the asparagus and blanch for 30 seconds to 1 minute, depending on the thickness; it should be tender but still crisp. Immediately drain the asparagus and rinse it with cold water. Set aside.

Place the lettuce in the bottom of a bowl and top with the blanched asparagus. Drizzle with the vinaigrette. Using the small holes of a grater, grate the hard-boiled egg over the asparagus. Season with salt and a few grinds of pepper.

Top with the chicken and goat cheese. Garnish with walnuts, dill, and lemon wedge.

This Week's Menu

Monday	GRILLED EGGPLANT AND POTATO SALAD BOWL
Tuesday	SMOKED SALMON FLATBREAD WITH FENNEL SALAD
Wednesday	SABICH FLATBREAD WITH POTATO SALAD
Thursday	FREEKEH BOWL WITH SMOKED SALMON
Friday	BABA GHANOUSH WITH FLATBREAD AND CHOPPED SALAD

This week, keep your phone handy at lunchtime, because you'll want to snap photos of these stunning bowls. Each is bursting with different colors and textures, making them worthy of the "foodporn" hashtag. Before you dismiss making your own flatbreads from scratch, please trust that they are super easy, extremely tasty, and so worth it. When you start enjoying them topped with smoked salmon, bright pink pickled onion, and crispy capers, you'll be really happy you put in the small amount of effort. Full of protein and fiber, freekeh is a variety of wheat that's harvested while it's young and then toasted, and it's an ideal base for any lunch bowl. If you can't find it near you, feel free to substitute either of its older siblings, farro or wheat berries.

Grocery List

Make sure you have the following ingredients for the week.

Pantry

¼ cup tahini

Extra virgin olive oil

Grapeseed oil

¾ cup white wine vinegar

1 tablespoon whole-grain mustard

1 tablespoon mayonnaise

¼ cup capers

1 (14-ounce) can white beans (cannellini, great northern, or similar)

1 cup freekeh (or wheat berries or farro)

1 (¼ ounce) packet dry active yeast

1 cup all-purpose flour, plus more for dusting

1 tablespoon dried thyme

1 tablespoon sesame seeds

¼ teaspoon cumin seeds

2 tablespoons sumac

4 black peppercorns (optional)

Produce

1 bunch chives

1 bunch dill

5 garlic cloves

1 small red onion

1½ pounds eggplant (about 1 large or 3 small eggplants)

1 pound baby potatoes

1 bulb fennel

2 lemons

2 (5-ounce) containers baby greens (kale, arugula, or similar)

2 Persian cucumbers

Dairy

1 egg

½ cup full-fat Greek yogurt

2 ounces feta cheese

Seafood

1 (4-ounce) package smoked salmon

Sunday Prep

Make the following recipes:

1 Tahini Sauce (see opposite)

2 Pickled Red Onions (see opposite)

3 Grilled Eggplant with Za'atar (page 181)

4 Potato Salad with Crispy Capers (page 182)

5 Marinated White Beans (page 183)

6 Yogurt Flatbreads (page 184)

Prepare and store in sealable containers in the refrigerator:

Freekeh: Bring a medium pot of salted water to a boil. Add 1 cup of freekeh and cook for 25 minutes. Drain and rinse with cold water. Makes about 2 cups of cooked freekeh.

Crispy capers: Drain ¼ cup of capers and pat dry with paper towels. In a small skillet over medium-high heat, heat 1 tablespoon of grapeseed oil. When the oil is hot, add the capers (be careful as they might sputter at first). Fry, shaking the pan, for 2 minutes, or until the capers are crispy. Line a bowl with paper towels and pour the capers into the bowl to drain.

7-minute egg: Bring a small saucepan of water to a boil. Using a spoon, carefully add the egg. Boil for 7 minutes. Rinse with cold water before storing.

Shaved fennel: Remove any bruised outer layers and reserve any bright green fronds. Cut the fennel in quarters and, using a mandoline or sharp knife, thinly shave the fennel. Store the fennel and fronds with a damp paper towel draped over them. Makes about 1 cup of shaved fennel.

Tahini Sauce

¼ cup tahini

1 small garlic clove, grated

Zest and juice of ½ lemon

Kosher salt

In a medium bowl, whisk the tahini with the garlic, lemon zest, and lemon juice. The mixture will be very thick. To thin it out, whisk in cold water, 1 tablespoon at a time, until the sauce is pourable. Season with salt to taste. Store in an airtight container in the refrigerator.

Pickled Red Onions

1 small red onion, thinly sliced

1 garlic clove

4 black peppercorns (optional)

½ cup white wine vinegar

1 teaspoon kosher salt

1 teaspoon sugar

Place the onion, garlic, and peppercorns (if using) in a small jar.

In a small saucepan over medium heat, heat the vinegar, salt, and sugar until the sugar has dissolved.

Pour the vinegar into the jar. If the onion slices aren't covered completely, add some hot water until they're just covered. Close the jar and store in the refrigerator.

Grilled Eggplant with Za'atar

☼ Makes 3 cups ☼

1 tablespoon dried thyme

1 tablespoon sesame seeds

1 garlic clove, grated

1 teaspoon kosher salt

¼ cup extra virgin olive oil

1 ½ pounds eggplant (about
1 large or 3 small eggplants)

Heat your grill to high. To make the za'atar, combine the thyme, sesame seeds, garlic, and salt in a small bowl. Add the oil, stir, and set aside.

Slice the eggplant into ¼-inch rounds. Place the rounds on a baking sheet and brush both sides with the za'atar mixture.

Place the eggplant slices on the hot grill and cook for 4 to 5 minutes on each side until you see nice charred grill marks. Transfer the eggplant to a baking sheet to cool before storing in an airtight container.

☼

tip ☼ **If you don't have access to a grill, you can cook these in a cast-iron pan or broil them in the oven.**

☼

Potato Salad with Crispy Capers

✿ Makes 3 cups ✿

¼ teaspoon kosher salt, plus more for boiling the potatoes

1 pound baby potatoes

1 tablespoon whole-grain mustard

1 tablespoon mayonnaise

1 tablespoon grapeseed oil

1 tablespoon white wine vinegar

1 tablespoon minced chives

½ teaspoon sumac

¼ cup thinly shaved fennel, plus some fronds

Small bunch dill, chopped

2 tablespoons crispy capers

Bring a medium saucepan of salted water to a boil. Add the potatoes and boil for 8 to 12 minutes, depending on the size of the potatoes, until they are fork-tender. Drain and let cool.

In a medium bowl, stir together the mustard, mayo, oil, vinegar, chives, salt, and sumac.

Cut all the potatoes in half (or in quarters if they're large) and add them to the bowl. Add the dressing, fennel, and dill and stir gently to combine. Top with the capers. Store in an airtight container in the refrigerator.

Marinated White Beans

✿ Makes 1½ cups ✿

⅓ cup extra virgin olive oil

¼ cup chopped chives

Torn dill fronds

2 tablespoons white wine vinegar

2 garlic cloves, lightly smashed

1 (14-ounce) can white beans (cannellini, great northern, or similar), drained and rinsed

Kosher salt

Black pepper

Combine the oil, chives, dill, vinegar, and garlic in a glass jar large enough to fit the beans. Set aside.

Place the beans in a small saucepan and cover with water. Bring to a boil, then immediately drain and transfer to the jar with the dressing. Season the beans with salt and pepper, then stir or shake to coat the beans with the marinade. Close the jar with the lid and store in the refrigerator.

Yogurt Flatbreads

✿ Makes 3 flatbreads ✿

1 teaspoon dry active yeast

½ teaspoon sugar

6 tablespoons warm water

1 cup all-purpose flour, plus more
for dusting

½ teaspoon kosher salt

2 tablespoons full-fat Greek yogurt

2 tablespoons extra virgin olive oil,
plus more for coating the bowl

3 teaspoons grapeseed oil

In a large bowl, combine the yeast, sugar, and water. Let sit for 5 minutes until frothy. Using a wooden spoon, stir in the flour and salt until a shaggy dough starts to form. Add the yogurt and olive oil, stir a few times, then switch to working with your hands and bring the dough together. Start to knead the dough in the bowl, adding flour if the dough sticks to the bowl or your hands. Knead for 2 minutes until the dough is smoother and more elastic and doesn't stick. Set the ball of dough aside and coat the bowl (it's okay if it's a little messy with flour) with some olive oil. Place the dough back in the oiled bowl, cover with plastic wrap or a dry kitchen towel, and set aside for 2 hours, or until the dough has doubled in size.

Heat a large cast-iron or nonstick skillet over medium-high heat. Divide the dough into 3 even pieces. One by one, roll each piece out on a well-floured surface into an ⅛-inch-thick round. Pour 1 teaspoon of grapeseed oil in the skillet and place 1 piece of dough in the skillet. Cook for 2 minutes on each side, without disturbing, until the flatbread starts to brown in spots. Transfer the flatbread to a plate or baking sheet and repeat with the remaining oil and dough.

Let the flatbreads cool and store them in a plastic bag or airtight container in the refrigerator. To reheat, place in a 350°F oven for 5 to 10 minutes until just warm.

Grilled Eggplant and Potato Salad Bowl

2 cups baby greens

½ cup cooked freekeh

1 tablespoon extra virgin olive oil

Kosher salt

¼ cup Marinated White Beans (page 183)

1 cup Potato Salad with Crispy Capers (page 182)

1 cup Grilled Eggplant with Za'atar (page 181)

1 ounce feta cheese

1 tablespoon Tahini Sauce (page 179)

Torn dill fronds

Minced chives

1 ½ teaspoons sumac

1 lemon wedge

Place the greens and freekeh in the bottom of a bowl. Drizzle with the oil and season with salt.

Top with the beans, potato salad, eggplant, and feta, and drizzle with the tahini sauce.

Garnish with dill, chives, sumac, and lemon wedge.

Smoked Salmon Flatbread with Fennel Salad

1 ½ cups baby greens

½ cup shaved fennel

¼ cup Marinated White Beans (page 183)

2 tablespoons full-fat Greek yogurt

1 Yogurt Flatbread (page 184), reheated in the oven

2 ounces smoked salmon

¼ cup Pickled Red Onions (page 179)

½ Persian cucumber, sliced

1 tablespoon crispy capers

Lemon zest

Torn dill fronds

Place the greens and fennel in the bottom of a bowl and top with the beans.

Schmear the yogurt on the flatbread and top with the salmon, onions, cucumber, and capers. Garnish with lemon zest and dill.

Place the flatbread on top of the salad.

TIP You can place a round piece of parchment paper between the salad and the flatbread to keep the bread from getting soggy.

Sabich Flatbread with Potato Salad

1 ½ cups baby greens

1 cup Potato Salad with Crispy Capers (page 182)

2 tablespoons full-fat Greek yogurt

1 Yogurt Flatbread (page 184), reheated in the oven

1 cup Grilled Eggplant with Za'atar (page 181)

One 7-minute egg, quartered

¼ cup Pickled Red Onions (page 179)

½ Persian cucumber, sliced

Kosher salt

2 tablespoons Tahini Sauce (page 179)

1 tablespoon crispy capers

Lemon zest

Torn dill fronds

1 ½ teaspoons sumac

Place the greens and potato salad in the bottom of a bowl.

Schmear the yogurt on the flatbread and top with the eggplant, egg, onions, and cucumber, and season with salt. Drizzle with the tahini sauce, top with the capers, and garnish with lemon zest, dill, and sumac.

Place the flatbread on top of the salad.

Freekeh Bowl with Smoked Salmon

1½ cups cooked freekeh

1 cup baby greens

1 tablespoon extra virgin olive oil

Kosher salt

¼ cup Marinated White Beans (page 183)

¼ cup Pickled Red Onions (page 179)

1 cup Potato Salad with Crispy Capers (page 182)

2 ounces smoked salmon

½ Persian cucumber, diced

2 tablespoons Tahini Sauce (page 179)

Torn dill fronds

Minced chives

2 teaspoons sumac

1 lemon wedge

Place the freekeh and greens in the bottom of a bowl. Drizzle with the oil and season with salt.

Add the beans, onions, potato salad, salmon, and cucumber. Drizzle with the tahini sauce and garnish with dill, chives, sumac, and lemon wedge.

Baba Ghanoush with Flatbread and Chopped Salad

1 cup Grilled Eggplant with Za'atar (page 181)

3 tablespoons extra virgin olive oil

2 tablespoons Tahini Sauce (page 179)

¼ teaspoon cumin seeds, lightly ground

¼ teaspoon kosher salt, plus more for seasoning

Zest and juice of 1 lemon

1 tablespoon minced chives

½ teaspoon sumac

3 cups baby greens

Any remaining Marinated White Beans (page 183)

¼ cup Pickled Red Onions (page 179)

½ Persian cucumber, diced

Dill fronds

1 ounce feta cheese, crumbled

1 Yogurt Flatbread (page 184), sliced

Make the baba ghanoush: Combine the eggplant, 2 tablespoons of oil, the tahini sauce, cumin seeds, salt, and half the lemon zest and juice in a blender or food processor and blend until smooth.

In the bottom of a bowl, combine the remaining 1 tablespoon of oil, the chives, the remaining half of the lemon juice and zest, sumac, and a pinch of salt.

Top with the greens, beans, onions, cucumber, dill, and feta. Toss gently to combine. Place the baba ghanoush on one side of the bowl and place the flatbread slices on the other.

This Week's Menu

Monday	ROSEMARY STEAK BOWL WITH ROASTED ARTICHOKES
Tuesday	CAPRESE SALAD WITH ROSEMARY STEAK AND BROCCOLI RABE
Wednesday	FARRO BOWL WITH SOPPRESSATA AND BROCCOLI RABE PESTO
Thursday	PANZANELLA SALAD WITH BURRATA AND PLUMS
Friday	FARRO AND QUINOA PORRIDGE WITH ROASTED PLUMS

The al fresco Italian lunch vibe of this week's recipes will have you dreaming of sunny, warm-weather outdoor lunches (and if you can, you should make those dreams a reality by taking your lunch outside). A fragrant Rosemary-Rubbed Steak is the centerpiece protein, complemented by a vibrant green Broccoli Rabe Pesto and creamy fresh mozzarella. After eating broccoli rabe throughout this week, it will become your go-to dark leafy green. It has all the same incredible nutritional value as other greens, as well as a distinctive, delightfully bitter flavor that comes alive when the rabe is cooked with olive oil and garlic. Before roasting your artichoke hearts, make sure to dry them really well to ensure maximum crispiness. The shopping list gives you the option of burrata or fresh mozzarella; if you haven't dipped into the burrata pool, trust me, this is the time. It's like regular mozzarella on the outside and incredibly creamy and rich on the inside; when burrata is torn into big pieces and dusted with some flaky sea salt it's the most glorious addition to any dish.

Grocery List

Make sure you have the following ingredients for the week.

Pantry

2 cups farro

¼ cup quinoa

Extra virgin olive oil

Grapeseed oil

½ teaspoon aged balsamic vinegar

2 tablespoons pure maple syrup

½ cup pine nuts

1 tablespoon chia seeds

1 (14-ounce) can artichoke hearts

½ teaspoon cinnamon

⅛ teaspoon cardamom

Red chili flakes

½ cup chicken stock (ideally homemade, page 18) or water

1 ciabatta roll

¼ cup (about 12) of your favorite olives, pitted

Flaky sea salt

Produce

4 garlic cloves

1 (1-inch) piece fresh ginger

1 bunch rosemary

1 bunch basil

1 bunch broccoli rabe

1 (5-ounce) container arugula or 2 bunches

3 heirloom tomatoes

1 Persian cucumber

1 plum

Dairy

¼ cup full-fat Greek yogurt

1 tablespoon butter

1 (8-ounce) ball burrata or fresh mozzarella

1 small block Parmigiano-Reggiano

1½ cups unsweetened almond milk

Meat

1 (1-pound) New York strip steak

10 to 15 thin slices soppressata (or similar dry cured salami)

Sunday Prep

Make the following recipes:

1 Rosemary-Rubbed Steak (see opposite)

2 Braised Broccoli Rabe (page 200)

3 Broccoli Rabe Pesto (page 200)

4 Roasted Artichoke Hearts (page 202)

Prepare and store in sealable containers in the refrigerator:

● Farro: In a medium saucepan, bring 3 cups of salted water to a boil. Add 2 cups of farro and continue to boil for 25 to 30 minutes until the farro is tender but still slightly chewy. Drain the farro and rinse it with cold water before storing. Makes about 4 cups of cooked farro.

● Cut the ciabatta roll into 1-inch cubes, and store in a plastic bag or container. Makes about 1 cup of cubed bread.

● Toasted pine nuts: Place the pine nuts in a small, dry skillet and turn the heat up to medium. Toast, shaking often, until the nuts become lightly golden brown.

Rosemary-Rubbed Steak

☼ Makes 2 servings (about 10 slices) ☼

1 sprig rosemary, leaves stripped and finely chopped

1 garlic clove, grated

1 tablespoon grapeseed oil, plus more for the grill

1 teaspoon kosher salt

Black pepper

1 (1-pound) New York strip steak

In a small bowl, mix the rosemary, garlic, oil, salt, and a few grinds of pepper. Rub the mixture all over the steak, transfer it to a plate, and let marinate in the refrigerator for at least 30 minutes and up to 4 hours.

Grill method: Heat your grill to high. Place the steak on the hottest part of the grill and cook for 4 minutes on each side, or until an instant-read thermometer inserted into the meat registers 135°F for rare and 140°F for medium-rare steak. Transfer the steak to a cutting board and let it rest for at least 5 minutes.

Cast-iron method: Heat the oven to 450°F. Heat a cast-iron pan over high heat. Once hot, place the steak in the pan and sear it for 30 seconds on each side. Transfer the pan to the oven and cook for 2 to 3 minutes, or until an instant-read thermometer inserted into the meat registers 135°F for rare and 140°F for medium-rare steak. Transfer the steak to a cutting board and let it rest for at least 5 minutes.

Once the steak has cooled down, cut it into ¼-inch-thick slices and store in an airtight container in the refrigerator.

Braised Broccoli Rabe

✿ Makes 2 cups ✿

---

3 tablespoons extra virgin olive oil

2 garlic cloves, sliced

Red chili flakes

1 bunch broccoli rabe, roughly chopped

½ cup chicken stock or water

In a large Dutch oven over medium heat, heat the oil, garlic, and red chili flakes. Cook the garlic for 2 minutes until it is soft but not browned.

Add the broccoli rabe and, using tongs, toss and coat it in the oil and cook for 1 minute. Pour in the stock, bring to a boil, reduce to a simmer, cover, and cook for 5 to 7 minutes until the broccoli rabe is wilted and tender. Store in an airtight container in the refrigerator.

Broccoli Rabe Pesto

✿ Makes ¾ cup ✿

½ cup Braised Broccoli Rabe

1 garlic clove

1 cup basil leaves

3 tablespoons toasted pine nuts

¼ cup extra virgin olive oil

¼ cup grated Parmigiano-Reggiano

1 teaspoon kosher salt

Place all the ingredients in a food processor or blender. Process until smooth, scraping down the sides with a rubber spatula once or twice. Store in an airtight container in the refrigerator.

Roasted Artichoke Hearts

✿ Makes 1 cup ✿

1 (14-ounce) can artichoke hearts, drained well

1 tablespoon grapeseed oil

Kosher salt

Black pepper

1 sprig rosemary

Heat the oven to 350°F. Using a paper towel, pat the artichoke hearts dry. Combine them with the oil, a pinch of salt, and a few grinds of pepper in a medium bowl.

Place the artichoke hearts on a baking sheet in one even layer and place the rosemary sprig on top.

Transfer the baking sheet to the oven and bake for 15 minutes, tossing the artichoke hearts once, until lightly browned and crispy. Store in an airtight container in the refrigerator.

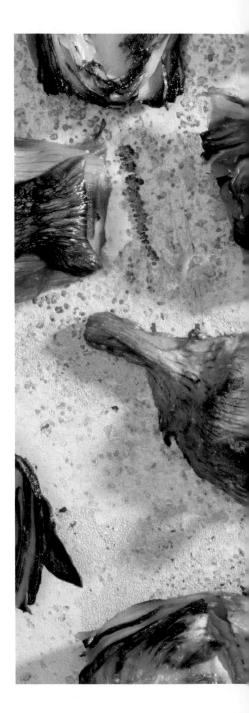

Rosemary Steak Bowl with Roasted Artichokes

2 cups arugula

½ cup cooked farro

¼ cup Broccoli Rabe Pesto (page 200)

½ cup Braised Broccoli Rabe (page 200)

½ cup Roasted Artichoke Hearts (page 202)

1 serving (5 slices) Rosemary-Rubbed Steak (page 199)

¼ cup (about 6) pitted olives

1 tablespoon toasted pine nuts

Torn basil leaves

Place the arugula and farro in the bottom of a bowl and drizzle with the pesto.

Top with the broccoli rabe, artichoke hearts, steak, and olives.

Garnish with the pine nuts and basil.

Caprese Salad with Rosemary Steak and Broccoli Rabe

2 cups arugula

½ teaspoon aged balsamic vinegar

½ teaspoon extra virgin olive oil

½ ball burrata, torn into big pieces

1 heirloom tomato, cut into wedges

½ cup Braised Broccoli Rabe (page 200)

1 serving (5 slices) Rosemary-Rubbed Steak (page 199)

Kosher salt

Black pepper

1 tablespoon toasted pine nuts

Torn basil leaves

Place the arugula in the bottom of a bowl and drizzle with the vinegar and oil.

Top with the burrata, tomato, broccoli rabe, and steak. Sprinkle with salt and a few grinds of pepper.

Garnish with the pine nuts and basil.

Farro Bowl with Soppressata and Broccoli Rabe Pesto

2 cups cooked farro

¼ cup Broccoli Rabe Pesto (page 200)

10 to 15 thin slices soppressata (or similar dry cured salami), cut into ¼-inch ribbons

1 heirloom tomato, diced

½ Persian cucumber, diced

½ cup Roasted Artichoke Hearts (page 202)

Torn basil leaves

¼ cup (about 6) pitted olives

Black pepper

Place the farro and pesto in the bottom of a bowl and stir together.

Top with the soppressata, tomato, cucumber, artichoke hearts, basil, and olives.

Garnish with a few grinds of black pepper.

Panzanella Salad
with Burrata and Plums

3 tablespoons extra virgin olive oil

1 cup cubed ciabatta bread

Kosher salt

1 cup arugula

1 heirloom tomato, cut into wedges

½ ball burrata, torn into big pieces

½ Persian cucumber, diced

½ plum, cut into wedges

¼ cup Broccoli Rabe Pesto (page 200)

1 tablespoon toasted pine nuts

Black pepper

Flaky sea salt

In a large skillet, heat the oil. Add the bread and cook over medium heat, tossing frequently, for 5 minutes, or until golden brown. Season with salt and set aside to cool.

Place the arugula, tomato, burrata, cucumber, and plum in the bottom of a bowl. Drizzle with the pesto, then top with the bread cubes.

Garnish with pine nuts, a few grinds of pepper, and flaky salt.

Farro and Quinoa Porridge with Roasted Plums

1½ cups unsweetened almond milk

1 cup cooked farro

¼ cup quinoa

2 rosemary sprigs

½ teaspoon cinnamon

1 (1-inch) piece fresh ginger, peeled and grated

⅛ teaspoon cardamom

Kosher salt

Black pepper

2 tablespoons pure maple syrup

1 tablespoon chia seeds

1 tablespoon butter

½ plum, cut into wedges

1 teaspoon extra virgin olive oil

½ teaspoon sugar

¼ cup full-fat Greek yogurt

2 tablespoons toasted pine nuts

Heat the oven to 350°F. Line a baking sheet with parchment paper or nonstick aluminum foil.

In a medium saucepan, bring the milk to a simmer. Add the farro, quinoa, 1 sprig of rosemary, the cinnamon, ginger, cardamom, a pinch of salt, and a few grinds of pepper. Simmer for 15 to 20 minutes, stirring often, until you get a thick, creamy porridge. Turn off the heat, discard the rosemary sprig, and stir in the maple syrup, chia seeds, and butter.

Meanwhile, place the plum wedges and the remaining rosemary sprig on the prepared baking sheet. Drizzle with the oil, sprinkle with the sugar, and toss lightly. Transfer to the oven and roast for 15 minutes until the fruit is tender and has caramelized slightly.

Place the porridge in a bowl, and top with the roasted plum, yogurt, and pine nuts.

Portable Treats

Cookies + Truffles + Crackers

Treats to Banish Your Cravings

For 10 chapters, we've solved the problem of having a satisfying lunch ready to dive into when that hunger pang hits. But after a few hours (or minutes), you'll be thinking about something sweet. We've all made the mistake of reaching for a super sugary treat, which appeased the sweet tooth in the moment but made us crash a few minutes later. Enter my recipes for treats! They're all sweetened with either pure maple syrup or honey and filled with goodness like nuts, ground flax seeds, and chia seeds, so these simple bites will give you a little energy boost to power you through the rest of the day. All of them are easy to make and can be stored in an airtight container at your desk or in the refrigerator. The last recipe in this chapter is a savory cracker, and it's meant to supplement any of the lunches in this book. You say, "Well, I can just buy a box of crackers to go with my lunch." That's true, but these crackers have only a few ingredients, all of which you can pronounce, and they come together so quickly. Why not have a homemade, quality snack that you can be super proud to show off . . . and possibly share.

Lemon and Olive Oil Cookies

✿ Makes 8 Cookies ✿

1 cup finely ground almond meal

2 tablespoons pure maple syrup

1 tablespoon extra virgin olive oil

Zest of ½ lemon

½ teaspoon vanilla extract

½ teaspoon almond extract (optional)

⅛ teaspoon baking powder

⅛ teaspoon kosher salt

Heat the oven to 350°F and place a rack in the middle position. Line a baking sheet with parchment paper. In a large bowl, mix all the ingredients using a rubber spatula. The dough should be thick and a little sticky.

Using a tablespoon measure, place rounded tablespoons of dough in your hand. Roll into a ball and place on the baking sheet. Using your fingers, press down on the ball to flatten it. Repeat with the remaining dough.

Bake the cookies for 10 to 12 minutes until the bottoms and edges are lightly browned. Let the cookies cool on the baking sheet before storing them in an airtight container.

Lime and Coconut Cookies

✿ Makes 8 Cookies ✿

¾ cup finely ground almond meal

¼ cup unsweetened shredded coconut

2 tablespoons pure maple syrup

1 tablespoon coconut oil, melted

Zest of ½ lime

½ teaspoon vanilla extract

⅛ teaspoon baking powder

⅛ teaspoon kosher salt

Heat the oven to 350°F and place a rack in the middle position. Line a baking sheet with parchment paper.

In a large bowl, mix all the ingredients using a rubber spatula. The dough should be thick and a little sticky.

Using a tablespoon measure, place rounded tablespoons of dough in your hand. Roll into a ball and place on the baking sheet. Using the spatula, press down on the dough to flatten it. Repeat with the remaining dough.

Bake the cookies for 10 to 12 minutes until the bottoms and edges are lightly browned. Let the cookies cool on the baking sheet before storing them in an airtight container.

Tahini and Apricot Truffles

✿ Makes 8 to 10 truffles ✿

½ cup rolled oats

1 tablespoon ground flax seeds

½ cup dried apricots

2 tablespoons tahini

2 tablespoons coconut oil, melted

1 tablespoon honey or pure maple syrup

¼ teaspoon vanilla extract

¼ teaspoon kosher salt

½ teaspoon ground cardamom

3 tablespoons sesame seeds (white, black, or a mix)

Place the oats and flax seeds in the bowl of a food processor. Blitz until a flour forms. Transfer to a large bowl and set aside.

Place the apricots, tahini, coconut oil, honey, vanilla, salt, and cardamom in the bowl of the food processor. Process until a chunky paste forms. Using a rubber spatula, transfer the mixture to the bowl with the flour, and stir until a crumbly wet mixture forms. You should be able to pinch the mixture together. (This is messy, but the coconut oil is great for your hands!)

Place the sesame seeds in a small bowl. Using your hands, roll the apricot mixture into 1-inch balls, then roll each ball in the sesame seeds and place on a plate. Transfer the balls to the refrigerator to chill for at least 30 minutes before eating. Store in an airtight container in the refrigerator.

Date and Chocolate Truffles

✿ Makes 8 to 10 truffles ✿

½ cup raw almonds, raw cashews, raw walnuts, or a mix

1 tablespoon ground flax seeds

2 tablespoons raw cacao powder

½ teaspoon cinnamon

¼ teaspoon kosher salt

1 tablespoon chia seeds

¾ cup Medjool dates, pitted

3 tablespoons coconut oil, melted

1 tablespoon pure maple syrup

2 ounces dark chocolate, chopped

Flaky sea salt

Place the nuts, flax seeds, cacao powder, cinnamon, and salt in the bowl of a food processor. Blitz until the nuts are finely ground. Transfer to a large bowl, add the chia seeds, and set aside. Place the dates, coconut oil, and maple syrup in the bowl of the food processor. Process until a chunky paste forms.

Using a rubber spatula, transfer the mixture into the bowl with the nut mixture, and stir until a crumbly wet mixture forms. You should be able to pinch the mixture together. Using your hands, form 1-inch balls and transfer them to a plate. Place in the refrigerator to chill.

Place the chocolate in a glass bowl and set over a small pan of simmering water, making sure the bottom of the bowl does not touch the water. Melting the chocolate this way, in a double boiler, ensures that it melts gently and won't separate or burn. (You can a melt the chocolate in the microwave at 30 second intervals, stirring in between.) Once the chocolate has melted, remove the pan from the heat.

Using your fingers, dip the top of one of the truffles into the chocolate, let the excess drip off and place the truffle back on the plate, chocolate side up. Sprinkle with a little flaky salt. Repeat with the remaining truffles, then return them to the refrigerator to chill for at least 20 minutes before eating. Store in an airtight container in the refrigerator.

Easy Herb Crackers

✿ Makes 10 to 15 crackers ✿

1 cup all-purpose flour, plus more for dusting

2 teaspoons dill, parsley, rosemary, or sage, finely chopped, or dried thyme, crumbled

1 teaspoon kosher salt

1 teaspoon sugar

Black pepper

2 tablespoons extra virgin olive oil

5 tablespoons cold water

Heat the oven to 450°F. Line a rimmed baking sheet with parchment paper.

In a large bowl, combine the flour, herbs, salt, sugar, and a few grinds of pepper. Add the oil and water. Using a fork, stir everything together until a shaggy dough forms. With clean hands, start to bring the dough together in the bowl and knead lightly for 1 minute.

Transfer the dough to a floured work surface and, using a rolling pin, roll out the dough as thin as you can. Using a knife or pizza cutter, cut the dough into bite-size pieces and place them on the baking sheet.

Bake for 8 to 10 minutes, until golden and crisp around the edges. Let the crackers cool, then store them in an airtight container.

Resources

My Favorite Spots in NYC

Dellapietras Brooklyn

This butcher shop has the best grass-fed, organic meats and poultry.

193 Atlantic Avenue, Brooklyn, NY 11201

Fish Tales

This neighborhood fishmonger is the place for the freshest, most delicious fish.

191A Court Street, Brooklyn, NY 11201
fishtalesonline.com

Kalustyan's

This is the mecca of spices, teas, and global foods. If you can't find it here, it probably doesn't exist.

123 Lexington Avenue, New York, NY 10016
foodsofnations.com

Sahadi's

A Middle Eastern specialty store, this Brooklyn favorite has the best selection of bulk items, olives, cheeses, and prepared foods.

187 Atlantic Avenue, Brooklyn, NY 11201
sahadis.com

Union Square Greenmarket

The flagship of New York's network of more than 50 markets has by far the most incredible array of seasonal foods and produce in the city. It is an ever-changing source of inspiration for many cooks, including me.

East 17th Street & Union Square West, New York, NY 10003
grownyc.org/greenmarket/manhattan-union-square

Whisk

With three locations in New York, this store has everything you may need for the kitchen, and maintains the mom and pop shop feel. They carry great knives, as well as a selection of jars and other storage containers.

197 Atlantic Avenue, Brooklyn, NY 11201
whisknyc.com

Online Resources

Crateandbarrel.com

If you only think of Crate and Barrel as a resource for furniture, think again. They have a great selection of stylish yet practical kitchen tools and kitchen storage solutions.

Gir.co

These incredibly well designed silicone kitchen tools take up some major real estate in my drawers. Their silicone storage lids fit bowls of any size and are reusable, and I love their silicone spatulas in all different sizes. Whatever your style, they've got a color for you.

Target.com

Everyone's favorite store! They always hit the mark when I'm looking for quality yet affordable kitchen supplies. Also, their grocery department is ever-expanding with organic food options.

Thrivemarket.com

There is an annual membership fee, but this market is filled with discounted health foods. The membership fee also helps fund free memberships for low income families. The website offers a free 30-day trial.

Wandpdesign.com

The Porter bowls, a beautiful line of portable lunch bowls used throughout this book, are available in a variety of colors on W&P's website, along with tons of beautiful and functional items for your kitchen and home.

Acknowledgments

I'd like to thank the whole team at Dovetail Press for giving me the opportunity to write such a fun cookbook. This book would never have come together so well without my editor, Mura Dominko, who spent hours helping me with each detail. Not only did I get an amazing book out of those lunch meetings, but I gained a close friend as well. My husband, Patrick, who is my consummate taste tester, idea springboard, and creative life partner. My dad and family, including Kerry and Bob, who have always supported my career and endeavors. And all my fellow stylists, photographers, and clients who have become friends and a constant source of inspiration and support.

Index

Note: Page numbers in *italics* refer to photographs.

C

D

Date and Chocolate Truffles, 219

E

Egg(s)
  Farro and Vegetable Bowl, 74
  hard-boiling, 158
  Kimchi Udon with an, 153
  Quinoa Bowl with a 6-Minute Egg, 44
  Quinoa Salad Niçoise, 54, *55*
  6-minute, 44
  7-minute, 62, 178
  Soba Noodle Soup, 91
  Soy Sauce Jammy, 86, *86–87*
  Soy Sauce, Spinach Salad with Sugar Snap Peas
    and, *92, 93*
Eggplant
  Baba Ghanoush with Flatbread and Chopped Salad,
    193
  Grilled, and Potato Salad Bowl, *186,* 187
  Grilled, with Za'atar, *180–181,* 181

F

Farro, 11
  Bowl with Chicken Skewers, 70, *71*
  Bowl with Soppressata and Broccoli Rabe Pesto, 208
  Porridge, and Quinoa, with Roasted Plums, *210,* 211
  Porridge with Yogurt and Caramelized Apples, *76, 77*
  preparing, 62, 198
  and Vegetable Bowl, 74
Fennel

Chicken Schnitzel with Caraway and, 164, *165*
  Salad, Smoked Salmon Flatbread with, 188, *189*
  shaving, 178
Fish. *See also* Salmon; Tuna
  marinating, 120
  Taco Bowl, *128,* 129
Flatbread(s)
  Baba Ghanoush with Chopped Salad and, 193
  Sabich, with Potato Salad, *190,* 191
  Smoked Salmon, with Fennel Salad, 188, *189*
  Yogurt, 184, *185*
Freekeh, 11
  Bowl with Smoked Salmon, 192
  Eggplant, Grilled, and Potato Salad Bowl, *186,* 187
  preparing, 178

G

Garlic Yogurt Sauce, 101
Ginger, 16
  Chicken Meatballs, 26, *26–27*
Goat Cheese, Chopped Salad with Shrimp, Asparagus
    and, 168, *169*

H

Halloumi
  Arugula Salad with Pickled Beets and Cucumbers, 53
  Quinoa Bowl with Carrot Slaw and, 50, *51*

I

ingredients
  pantry staples, 11–15

About the Author

Olivia Mack McCool is a food stylist and recipe developer based in Brooklyn. Her work, influenced by her training at Le Cordon Bleu in Paris and the colorful food scene of New York City, has appeared in cookbooks, magazines, and ad campaigns. When she's not on set or writing, she is still in the kitchen cooking for her friends and family.